D1624976

Society in Colonial North Carolina

Meclinbrugh october 23 1771

Loveing sister we are in good health at present
thanks be to god for all his mercys to us I
long to hear from you I cannot give you an
acount of our proceedings on the road
except I was with you I am as well
satisfid here as I can be any where in
the circumstance I am in our freinds
are all kind to us I desire it as a favour
from you to send me an acount of that
calico you were present when disant
got it he says he lost the invoice I have
wrote to brother mark if he does not send
it I will go for it if god spares me life
an health if you send any thing to me
send as much purple calico as will make
a gown for hannah an a little camrick
an lawn Just what sort you please I
hope mark will be as good as his word
about comeing out the bearer can inform
you better about this contry then I can I am
obliged to you for your past favours in parti
cular for the provision you sent with us my best
respects to brother mark an cox
    I am your Loving sister priscilla white
for mary cox

In a letter dated 1771 Priscilla White of Mecklenburg County requested her
sister Mary Cox of Baltimore to send an invoice for calico purchased earlier.
Mrs. White wrote, "I am as well-satisfied here as I could be anywhere in the
circumstance I am in . . . send as much purple calico as will make a gown for
Hannah an a little cambrick an lawn just what sort you please."

Society in Colonial North Carolina

by

Alan D. Watson

Alan D. Watson (signature)

Raleigh
North Carolina Department of Cultural Resources
Division of Archives and History
1975

Copyright, 1975, by the North Carolina Division of
Archives and History

DEPARTMENT OF CULTURAL RESOURCES

Mrs. Grace J. Rohrer

Secretary

DIVISION OF CULTURAL RESOURCES

Robert E. Stipe

Director

Larry E. Tise

Assistant Director

NORTH CAROLINA HISTORICAL COMMISSION

T. Harry Gatton

Chairman

c.2

CONTENTS

Maps and Illustrations

FOREWORD

For many years the Division of Archives and History has published pamphlets for schoolchildren and adults interested in North Carolina history. A wide variety of topics has been selected, and the timespan has stretched from the days of the Regulators through the years of World War II. It is with pleasure that Dr. Alan D. Watson's new pamphlet, *Society in Colonial North Carolina*, is being published as another in a well-established series of short, illustrated booklets.

Dr. Watson, associate professor of history at the University of North Carolina at Wilmington, is a native of Rocky Mount. His master's degree is from East Carolina University and his Ph.D. from the University of South Carolina. He is the author of a number of articles published in the *South Carolina Historical Magazine* and in the *North Carolina Historical Review*. His knowledge of colonial history makes him exceptionally well qualified to write on North Carolina life during the years preceding the American Revolution.

Mrs. Mary Reynolds Peacock, historical publications editor in the Historical Publications Section, edited the manuscript and saw it through the press. It was she who obtained illustrations for the pamphlet and wrote the cutlines. The manuscript was typed and prepared in camera-ready form by Miss Kathy Williamson, formerly on the staff of the Historical Publications Section; final details of page makeup were handled by Mrs. Henri Dawkins, currently on the staff.

Memory F. Mitchell
Historical Publications
Administrator

February 3, 1975

CHAPTER I

SETTLEMENT

Although North Carolina was the scene of two attempted settlements in 1585 and 1587 sponsored by Sir Walter Raleigh, the colony did not receive its first permanent white inhabitants until the 1650s. Those early colonists came not from England or the European continent but from Virginia and settled in the Albemarle region to establish a fur trade with the Indians of that area. In 1663 Charles II of England granted land including North Carolina to eight prominent Englishmen who had assisted the king in his exile and aided his accession to the throne.

The Reſtauration of Monarchy &
KING CHARLES II.

Charles II (1630-1685) experienced a decade of hardship and exile from his homeland before he ascended the throne of England in 1660 and was formally crowned in 1661. Although he was called the "Merrie Monarch," Charles was seriously interested in the welfare of his empire. His reign was notable as a period of great progress in many areas, especially in science, commerce, and the arts. Restoration picture supplied by Mr. William S. Powell, Chapel Hill; portrait photograph from the files of Division of Archives and History.

The Albemarle remained the center of settlement throughout the proprietary era. Efforts by a group of Barbadians and Low Englanders to establish a colony along the lower Cape Fear between 1664 and 1667 proved abortive. However, resident North Carolinians and immigrants gradually moved southward to the Pamlico and Neuse rivers. The establishment of Bath in 1705, the de Graffenried settlement at New Bern in 1710, and the incorporation of the town of Beaufort in 1723 reflected that activity. The Cape Fear enterprise of the Moore brothers in the 1720s finally inaugurated permanent settlement of the southeastern part of the province.

When the crown purchased North Carolina from the proprietors in 1729, the colony contained approximately 36,000 inhabitants. Their numbers included some 1,000 Indians and 6,000 blacks. The whites were a diverse people. English predominated but Welsh, French, Swiss, German Palatines, and Scotch-Irish composed minority groups; in addition, there were individual Lowland Scots. The Welsh colonized an area on the Northeast Cape Fear River which was known as the Welsh Tract. The French were Huguenots (Protestants) from Virginia who arrived as early as 1690 or 1691 to settle near the head of the Pamlico River. Another group of Huguenots planted on the Trent River in the first decade of the eighteenth century. The Swiss and Germans arrived principally with the de Graffenried expedition while the Scotch-Irish came to North Carolina as indentured servants.

White settlers of English origin comprised about eighty percent of the white population. They came to North Carolina from England, other North American mainland colonies, and the West Indies to find cheaper and more fertile land, a more temperate climate, religious toleration, and freedom from political restraint. Population during the proprietary period exhibited a slow but steady increase, though it was rudely interrupted by the Tuscarora Indian War from 1711 to 1714 in which many lives were lost.

After the purchase of North Carolina by the crown, the population of the colony rose markedly. The provincials numbered between 65,000 and 75,000 in 1750 and between 175,000 and 185,000 in 1770. Although the high birthrate of Carolinians contributed to the rapid rise in population, immigration principally explained the five-fold increase in settlers during the royal era.

Observations concerning the extraordinary influx of settlers emanated from sources within North Carolina and from outside the colony. Gov. Gabriel Johnston in 1751 reported numerous people immigrating to the colony, and three years later Gov. Arthur Dobbs told English authorities that hundreds of wagons had entered North Carolina from the northern colonies. Virginia minister James Maury wrote that during 1755 over 5,000 Virginians had crossed the James River headed for North Carolina and that 300 had passed the Bedford County courthouse in one week during 1756.

By terms of the charter pictured above Charles II in 1663 granted to the eight Lords Proprietors the New World territory known as Carolina. In 1729 Carolina became a royal colony when seven of the Lords Proprietors sold the property to George II, then king of England. George Carteret was the only one who refused to sell his holdings to the king. From the files of the North Carolina Division of Archives and History.

The rate of immigration continued unabated in the 1760s. Benjamin Franklin in 1763 wrote that some 10,000 families had moved from Pennsylvania to North Carolina in the preceding decade. And in 1766 Gov. William Tryon erred little when he stated that North Carolina's rate of settlement was greater than that of any other colony. In fact, only Georgia, which had started from a much smaller base population, exceeded North Carolina's population growth rate. Although some immigrants settled the remaining vacant land in the eastern counties, the majority planted in the western regions of the colony, which led a Virginia newspaper to report that "There is scarce any history, either antient [sic] or modern, which affords an account of such a rapid and sudden increase" of population.

The new colonists represented diverse nationalities, languages, social classes, and economic groups. While the English constituted the preponderance of the immigrants, the Scottish Highlanders, Scotch-Irish, and Germans composed significant minority stocks. The Scots who came to North Carolina after 1730 were "the earliest, largest, and most numerous settlement of Highlanders in America." More interested in joining relatives or friends than in seeking western land, the Scots were the only large, non-English nationality to come directly from their native land. The migration from Scotland to North America began after the Act of Union in 1707, continued throughout the remainder of the colonial era, and peaked in the early 1770s. Economic distress and political retribution in the wake of Scottish defeat in the Battle of Culloden in 1746 were the major stimuli prompting the Scots to come to America.

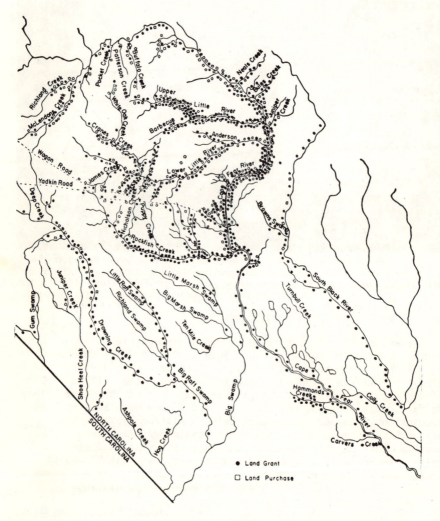

This map of land grants and sales to the Highlanders, 1733-1775, is reproduced from Duane Meyer, *The Highland Scots of North Carolina* (Raleigh: Carolina Charter Tercentenary Commission, 1963), 34.

The number of Highlander immigrants before 1763 is impossible to determine. Between the end of the French and Indian War and the beginning of the Revolution approximately 25,000 Scots left their homeland. More than 5,000 came to North Carolina. Fifty-four ship-loads of Scots arrived in the colony in the summer of 1770 alone. By 1775 the estimated number of Scots in the province ranged from 10,000 to 20,000.

The Scot immigrants included both Highlanders and Lowlanders. The latter were far less numerous but disproportionately important because they included many merchants who played a significant role in the colonial economy. The Lowlanders scattered throughout the province but the clan-conscious Highlanders concentrated in a well-defined area in the upper Cape Fear Valley which comprised the counties of Anson, Bladen, Cumberland, Harnett, Hoke, Moore, Richmond, Robeson, Sampson, and Scotland. Subsequently they extended their settlements westward to the land between the Catawba and Yadkin rivers.

The Scotch-Irish, Scots or decendants of Scots who had settled in Ireland, emigrated for various reasons. The Woolens Act of 1699 dealt a severe blow to that industry in Ireland, the Test Act of 1704 militated against the unlimited practice of Presbyterianism, and excessive rents for farms and widespread famines caused distress in the rural areas. A Pennsylvania newspaper in 1729 referred to the inhabitants of Ulster when it stated that "Poverty, wretchedness, misery, and want are become almost universal among them."

Although most colonies received some Scotch-Irish, Pennsylvania was the most popular due to its fertile land and tolerant religious policies. From the Pennsylvania entrepôt the Scotch-Irish fanned out through the Appalachian foothills and valleys. They utilized the "Great Wagon Road" which began at the Schuylkill opposite Philadelphia, ran westward through Lancaster to the Susquehanna River, then wended through the Shenandoah Valley in Virginia to Staunton Gap, crossed the Dan River in North Carolina, and terminated at the Yadkin River at which point other roads spread through western North Carolina and into South Carolina. Some Scotch-Irish chose to enter North Carolina from the south. They disembarked at Charleston and followed the trading routes from that port to the backcountry to reach the northern province.

The Germans followed the Scotch-Irish route to the Piedmont of North Carolina. Although they represented various religious denominations, the Germans generally regarded themselves as a distinct group in the province and proved more zealous in confining their settlements to western North Carolina then any other group of immigrants. Religious, political, and economic distress forced thousands of Germans to flee their native lands in the early 1700s. Some who came to North Carolina sought cheaper land; others intended to establish self-contained communal villages. The Moravians exemplified the latter. Their tract of land of almost 100,000 acres, known as Wachovia, was settled in 1753. The North Carolina colony was an extension of the Pennsylvania Moravian group wherein the brethren practiced communal ownership of property and mutual cooperation.

Supplementing the white immigrants were the blacks who generally bore the status of slaves. The black population was concentrated in the eastern counties of the province, particularly Perquimans, Chowan, and Gates in the northeast and New Hanover, Brunswick, and present-day Pender in the southeast. The number of blacks multiplied primarily by natural increase rather than by immigration after 1763. Before that year the slave population ranged from one fifth to one sixth of the white population. After 1763 the percentage gradually increased until the 1790 census placed the black population at slightly more tnan 25 percent of the total inhabitants of the state.

A map showing the direction taken by prospective settlers from Pennsylvania going into the southern and southwestern colonies appeared in the *Iron Worker*, XXXVII, No. 1 (Winter, 1973), 8, to illustrate an article by Parke Rouse, Jr., who wrote, "The most important frontier road in colonial America was the trail forged principally by Scotch-Irish and Germanic settlers from Philadelphia southward through the Appalachians to Georgia, known as the Great Wagon Road." Photograph used by permission of Lynchburg Foundry Company. ("The Iron Worker" is a registered trademark of the Lynchburg Foundry Company, a Mead Company. Contents copyrighted 1973 by Lynchburg Foundry Company, A Mead Company.)

CHAPTER II

CHARACTER AND CLASS

The general character of North Carolinians is difficult to determine from the conflicting assessments given by eighteenth century observers. John Brickell concluded that Carolinians were tall, straight, and active people who were discreet, thrifty, and industrious. The women usually avoided exposure to the weather but they too were diligent and unusually expert at their household duties.

On the other hand, William Byrd's derogatory evaluation must be recognized. According to this aristocratic Virginian, North Carolina deliberately encouraged debtors and criminals to immigrate to the colony in order to augment its population. In an entry made in his diary for March 25, 1729, Byrd continued his exaggerated description in the following manner:

> The Men, for their Part, just like the Indians, impose all the Work upon the poor Women. They make their Wives rise out of their Beds early in the Morning, at the same they lye and Snore, till the Sun has run one third of his course, and disperst all the unwholesome Damps. Then, after Stretching and Yawning for half an Hour, they light their Pipes, and under the Protection of a cloud of Smoak, venture out into the open Air; tho', if it happens to be never so little cold, they quickly return Shivering into the Chimney corner. When the weather is mild they stand leaning with both their arms upon the corn-field fence, and gravely consider whether they had best go and take a Small Heat at the Hough: but generally find reasons to put it off till another time.
> Thus they loiter away their Lives, like Solomon's Sluggard, with their Arms across, and at the Winding up of the Year Scarcely have Bread to Eat.
> To speak the Truth, tis a thorough Aversion to Labor that makes People file off to N Carolina, where Plenty and a Warm Sun confirm them in their Disposition to Laziness for their whole Lives.

Obviously the true character of Carolinians lay between the observations of Brickell and Byrd. In the East the colonials were a relatively indolent people due to a number of factors including the ease of producing food and raising livestock, the warm climate, and the use of slaves. Moreover, their appearance often connoted the reverse of vigor and strength. They were tall and lean, short-waisted and long-limbed, sallow-complexioned and languid-eyed.

Flat feet and loose joints contributed to an uneven walk. In the West, however, the people were bold and resourceful with impressive athletic ability. Many lived in the manner of Indians and were acknowledged by the Indians to be exceptionally skilled in the lore and ways of the woods.

Although the English mainland colonies in general and North Carolina in particular were quite democratic by eighteenth century standards, society was nevertheless structured into a hierarchy of classes. At least three classes characterized the white social order: the gentry, the middle class, and the lower or "meaner" sort of people. The gentry, composed of the leading planters, merchants, and professional men, was the smallest of the three groups. Members of that class were distinguished by superior wealth, education, and sophistication in worldly affairs. The gentry lived elegantly, at least by North Carolina standards, and provided political as well as social and cultural leadership for the colony.

The middle and lower classes constituted the most numerous segments of the populace. The former consisted primarily of small-er farmers and merchants, less prestigious professional men, and town artisans. The lower order included the very poor farmers, tenant farmers, day laborers, and similar dependent members of society. The life-styles of the middle and lower orders betrayed their inferior wealth and breeding. They were kind, hospitable, and generous; yet they were also rude, noisy, and uncouth.

Below the three primary classes and outside the prevailing social structure lay the indentured servants and slaves. Indentured servants fell into two classes: voluntary and non-voluntary. The former were "redemptioners," poor people who bound themselves to a labor contract for three to five years in order to pay their passage to America. The non-voluntary servants were paupers, convicts, and political prisoners who were shipped by the English authorities to the colonies where they were sold under similar contracts of slightly longer duration. While serving their masters the servants enjoyed a status little better than that of chattel slavery. However, they did possess some civil rights and their contracts did direct their masters to educate the servants and teach them a trade. At the end of the period of indenture masters were required to give the servants "freedom dues" which consisted variously of barrels of corn, suits of clothes, guns, or money.

Slaves represented the nadir of the provincial social system. As a form of property slaves were subject completely to the will of their masters. Not until 1774 was there legislation to prevent the purposive slaying of a slave, and the penalty for the first offense was only twelve months imprisonment. Every apparent aspect of the lives of the slaves--food, clothing, shelter, marriage, travel, work, leisure--from their birth or importation depended upon their owners' inclination. And one of the most piti-

Slave quarters in an unidentified location were pictured by Mrs. Bayard Wootten and used in Alex Matthews Arnett, *The Story of North Carolina* (Chapel Hill: University of North Carolina Press, 1933), 287.

ful scenes in the province was the slave auction block where humans were examined like animals and families including young children were separated forever.

Despite the authoritarian structure within which they lived, the slaves often managed to create their own society. Marriages were arranged and approved by masters but slaves managed to enjoy private family relationships. Under adverse circumstances male slaves often dominated and disciplined their families. Religious activities quickly became important to them. Slaves also enjoyed their own forms of recreation including dancing, singing, and games. Masters came to respect the limitations of slave endurance, inasmuch as the price of ignoring customary Sunday and Christmas holidays, for example, was likely to be work slowdowns, broken agricultural implements, and abused animals.

For many slaves the burden of bondage became unbearable. Advertisements for the recovery of runaway slaves filled the newspapers. Descriptions by the owners indicated the white attitude toward those slaves bold enough to challenge the slave system. Runaways were termed surly, cunning, artful, and flippant. At the same time the advertisements showed that many slaves had overtly protested their enslavement. The back of one runaway evidenced the frequent discipline of the whip; another had recently suffered a broken arm due to a blow received at the elbow. Many of the runaways made good their escape while others purposely committed suicide rather than return to their bondage.

Occupying an uncertain position in society between free whites, bondservants, and slaves were the free blacks. The origins of free blacks were many. Some were runaway slaves, mostly from other provinces, who passed for free persons in North Carolina. William Byrd and his surveying party found a family of blacks who "call'd themselves free, tho' by the Shyness of the Master of the House, who took care to keep least in Sight, their Freedom seem'd a little Doubtful." Slaves who were freed by will, deed, or legislative prescription constituted another source of free blacks. Faithful or meritorious service prompted most of the liberations although free blacks often purchased wives, children, and relatives in order to free them. The children of miscegenation (racially mixed unions) greatly added to the number of free blacks. Such offspring took the status of their mothers, and innumerable instances occurred in which white women bore the children of black, often slave, men.

The legal discriminations against free blacks were numerous. Their right to vote was restricted. They could not testify in court against whites and were probably excluded from jury duty. Still, the free blacks bore the same responsibilities to defend and support the government. They were liable for militia duty and work on the public roads. Free blacks also labored under an excessive tax burden. Wives, black and white, as well as female children of free black males were subject to taxation unlike wives and female children of whites. The inordinate tax burden provoked protests from many residents, including whites, of Granville, Edgecombe, and Northampton counties; but effective reform did not materialize.

The concept of class distinction readily appealed to North Carolinians since they originated in Europe where hierarchical societies prevailed. The structured society was reinforced in the colony by the Fundamental Constitutions, the document proposed by the proprietors for the governance of North Carolina. The Constitutions attempted unsuccessfully to establish a type of feudal society in the province. Social institutions such as orphanages also contributed to the practice of class distinction. According to law orphans had to be educated according to their rank and degree in society.

Class lines were not rigid, however. Economic opportunities in the new and expanding province offered avenues to quick riches which could lead to an elevation of social status. Constant fraternizing by Carolinians of all classes tended to blur class distinctions. Colonials mingled amiably at court sessions, church services, taverns, and sporting events. In fact, North Carolina was considered one of the most democratic English colonies in America, a province in which the "leveling spirit" was far advanced. Possibly the geographic situation of the colony between the aristocratic provinces of Virginia and South Carolina helped to accentuate North Carolina's democratic tendencies.

CHAPTER III

LIFE-STYLE

General Description of Colonial Household

The construction and adornment of colonial homes depended upon the geographical location of the structures and most especially upon the wealth of the builders. Typically the homes were log cabins, wooden frame dwellings, and brick houses. And the variety of structures renders a general account of the homes as difficult as a similar account of American homes today.

The poorer element of society, particularly in the newly settled regions of the colony, often lived in houses of log construction. Many were one-room buildings with lofts and sheds or lean-tos for additional space. Popular variations included the double cabin or two cabins under one roof. The saddle-bag plan attached two buildings on either side of a single chimney. The dog-run or possum-trot plan separated two cabins by an open breezeway which permitted ventilation, storage, and protected play.

The Robert Cleveland log house in Wilkes County near Purlear is pictured above. This one is unusual in that it is two-storied with a massive stone chimney at each end. Photograph by Tony Vaughn supplied by the Survey Unit, Division of Archives and History.

The Brothers' House in Salem is a good example of a half-timbered, brick-filled construction. This was a type used in Europe throughout the seventeenth century but rare in North Carolina. The structure appears in the background of the John Clymer painting which depicts a July, 1783, Independence Day celebration. Photograph courtesy of the American Cyanamid Company.

William Byrd, while surveying the boundary between Virginia and North Carolina in 1728, observed that most of the houses were constructed of logs which were mortised together and covered with pine or cypress shingles. Doors swung on wooden hinges and were secured by wooden locks. Thus, neither nails nor any other ironwork was necessary.

Houses with wooden frames or skeletons represented a European tradition of building which dated from medieval times. These houses might be part timber and part brick, weatherboard or clapboard, part timber with plaster, or tile hung. The Brothers' House in Old Salem, dating from 1769, exemplifies the half-timbered house with brick filling. The Cupola House in Edenton, dating from the mid-1720s, is one of the oldest remaining frame houses in North Carolina. The house is notable for its cupola and for its overhanging second story, which is a feature of Jacobean architecture.

Brick houses were reserved for the wealthy and conveyed a sense of power, if not elegance. Colonial architects cleverly designed the brick to create numerous patterns from glazed and darker and lighter bricks. Interestingly, the mortar often contained pieces of shells since the colonials made their lime from oyster

Built ca. 1724-1726, the Cupola House in Edenton was bought in 1756 by Francis Corbin, land agent of Lord Granville. In 1777 it was purchased by a prominent physician, Samuel Dickinson, whose descendants eventually sold the house to its present owners, the Cupola House Association. From the files of the Division of Archives and History.

and other shells. An eminent example of colonial brick construction is Tryon's Palace in New Bern which has been restored for the public. The Palace was built for the residence of the governor, and its great expense contributed to political unrest in the western areas of the colony. The mansion was hardly completed before being abandoned by Gov. Josiah Martin in 1775 and partially destroyed thereafter by the Carolinians.

Apart from the simple one-room log cabins and rudimentary frame houses, the floor plans of the houses differed markedly. Two-room houses consisted of a living room-kitchen combination and bedroom. Three-room structures utilized the same idea but with the bedroom divided for more privacy. Often halls separated the living room and bedrooms for greater privacy, particularly when the halls led to the loft or attic above which also served as a bedroom as well as storage area.

The two-story design found in the Piedmont was probably brought by the Quakers from the northern provinces. Russellborough, located just north of Brunswick Town and the home of Governors Dobbs and Tryon, represented a fine example of such a house in the East. Tryon left an excellent description of the house:

The House . . . is of an oblong Square Built of Wood. It measures on the out Side Faces forty five feet by thirty five feet, and is Divided into two Stories, exclusive of the Cellars the Parlour Floor is about five feet above the Surface of the Earth. Each Story has four Rooms and three light Closets. The Parlour below & the drawing Room are 20 x 15 feet each; Ceilings low. There is a Piaza Runs Round the House both Stories of ten feet Wide with a Ballustrade of four feet high, which is a great Security for my little girl.

Foundation remains of the Hepburn-Reonalds House in Brunswick Town continue to fascinate modern archaeologists; a conjectural drawing of the house by D. Mayhew appears in the lower photograph. Copied from John V. Allcott, *Colonial Homes in North Carolina* (Raleigh: Carolina Charter Tercentenary Commission, 1963), 75.

14

Old Town Plantation, thought to be the oldest house still standing in Edgecombe County, was built in 1742 by Samuel Holliman. Especially notable features include its gambrel roof, its wide, pegged weatherboards, its English-bond foundation and Flemish-bond chimneys. Photograph from the files of the Division of Archives and History and used in Alan D. Watson, "Colonial Edgecombe County," *North Carolina Historical Review*, L (Summer, 1973), 232.

Lillington Hall, home of John Alexander Lillington, was built in 1734, near the Wilmington-New Bern road, on the northeast branch of the Cape Fear River, about thirty miles above Wilmington; it no longer exists, however. Photograph from an engraving pictured in Benson J. Lossing, *The Pictorial Field-Book of the American Revolution: or, Illustrations, Scenery, Relics, and Traditions of the War of Independence* (New York: Harper and Brothers, 2 volumes, 1851-1852), II, 381.

The Old Brick House, so named because of its brick-end construction, is located in Elizabeth City, Pasquotank County, and presently owned by Mr. and Mrs. John M. Stuart. It is thought to have been built by Robert Murden (Munden) shortly after he bought the lot on which it stands from Isaac Stokely in 1750. In nominating the house for inclusion in the National Register of Historic Places it was noted that "the extent and quality of the interior elaboration of both [the Old Brick House and the Cupola House] suggests that they were considered mansions in comparison to standard residences of the region." Photograph from the Department of Natural and Economic Resources.

Bellair, home of Mr. and Mrs. G. Tull Richardson, is located in Craven County. The original construction of this fine home is dated at ca. 1772; it was begun by Richard Spaight, probably soon after his marriage to Elizabeth Wilson in 1756. William Blount, later owner, finished the east wing, 1789-1799. Photograph by Tony Vaughn, courtesy of the Survey Unit, Division of Archives and History.

Prosperous John Burgwin owned the two houses depicted. In the top is his Wilmington house, now called the Burgwin-Wright House; the formal garden at the rear is a notable feature. (Photograph by Southeastern Engraving Company, Wilmington, and reproduced from Donald R. Lennon and Ida Kellam, *The Wilmington Town Book* [Raleigh: Division of Archives and History, 1973], 157.) The home called Hermitage once existed on Burgwin's Castle Hayne plantation. Photograph of an etching reproduced in *Magazine of American History*, Volume 16, 1886.

Numerous outbuildings surrounded many of the houses. In the more primitive houses cooking was done in the house, while in some of the more elaborate houses the kitchen was in the cellar beneath the house. But often the kitchens were detached from the houses because of the danger of fire. The range of additional outbuildings included well houses, smokehouses, dairies, coach houses, privies, and barns.

Ornamental gardens complemented the homes of the wealthy who could afford the leisure and expense of such luxuries. Gardens not only represented beauty to those who appreciated the aesthetics of nature but also an attempt to imitate the contemporary European gentry and thus secure corresponding social prominence in America. The gardens of John Burgwin, Cape Fear merchant and politician, at his plantation north of Wilmington, The Hermitage, encompassed three acres. A creek wound through the largest garden. A fishpond was linked to the creek and both contained an abundance of fish. The garden contained several alcoves, summerhouses, and a hothouse as well as the family chapel. A second ornamental garden and the vegetable or "cook's" garden also complemented The Hermitage.

In terms of size and value beds, other large furniture, and kitchen utensils constituted the bulk of the furnishings in the average colonial household. Feather beds were the most popular item and represented an element of wealth in the home. Flock beds--mattresses stuffed with woolen or cotton refuse, rags, corn husks, or other material--were less desirable alternatives. Cradles and trundle beds were used for children, with the trundle beds neatly slipped under the larger beds in the day and brought out for use at night.

The colonials used the word "bed" to describe the mattress. The bedsteads and bed "furniture" were separate items. Bedsteads were wooden frames with a cord laced back and forth to support the mattress. The wealthy had elaborate headboards and four-poster bedsteads with hanging curtains surrounding the bed for warmth, protection, and privacy. The "furniture" accompanying the bed included such curtains, as well as pillows, sheets, blankets, rugs (bedrugs, heavier than blankets), coverlets, quilts, and comforters.

Larger furniture other than the beds was kept to a minimum because the houses were generally small. Trunks and chests were tucked away in corners. Chests of drawers, safes, and cupboards also served for storage. The more commodious houses were furnished with a varying number and style of tables and chairs, leather couches, and desks of mahogany, walnut, maple, and pine.

In the homes in which the cooking was conducted in the house, the kitchen with its huge fireplace dominated the interior. Beside the hearth were fire shovels, tongs, and one or more box irons and heaters or warming pans. An enormous variety of cooking utensils cluttered the fireplace and its surroundings. At the mouth of the chimney hung pothooks and racks. Andirons stood on the floor. Iron, brass, and copper kettles and pots rested near, accompanied by skillets, frying pans, saucepans, skimmers, ladles, and flesh forks. For use in the preparation of food, colanders, pattypans, handmills, sifters, graters, and various items of woodenware were available.

Food was eaten in close proximity to the kitchen. Tables were used where available, and the wealthy owned fine tablecloths. The less affluent used cloths of simple materials or improvised. Most colonials possessed the usual complement of knives, forks, and spoons and ate from dishes, plates, trenchers, and porringers which were generally pewter but often stone, wood, or earthenware. Wealthy families sometimes owned fine silver and china. Bowls, tureens, cups, mugs, and tumblers--also made from diverse materials-- served to hold liquids. In the vicinity of the kitchen were kept bottles of various kinds and sizes, pepperboxes, mustard pots, and butter pots; salt cellars often served as the centerpieces for colonial tables.

This photograph of the Joel Lane House in Raleigh affords a glimpse of the interior of a relatively simple house furnished in the colonial style. (From Allcott, *Colonial Homes in North Carolina*, 93.) Below is pictured the dining room of the Powell Satterthwaite House in Edgecombe County. The house was built ca. 1770, and the room is now on display in the Museum of Early Southern Decorative Arts, Old Salem. (Courtesy, Museum of Early Southern Decorative Arts, Winston-Salem, N.C.)

A log building reassembled and furnished in the colonial manner is used as the Old Fort Visitor Center. Note the rope bed, hand-loomed coverlet, the butter churn at far right, the bellows, and other accouterments of a colonial kitchen. (Photograph by Bob Allen.) Even the kitchen at Tryon Palace, pictured below, was furnished with similar utensils. Such refinements as the trestle table were unusual, however. Photographs from the files of the Division of Archives and History.

Pewter, china, and tableware from the colonial period are pictured on display at the North Carolina Museum of History. Photograph from the files of the Division of Archives and History.

Archaeologists digging at Halifax in recent years have unearthed artifacts of colonial utensils, some of which are pictured here. Photograph by Stuart C. Schwartz.

Indian influence on the customs and life-style of colonists is evident in the pictured utensils made from gourds and reeds, which were readily available in North Carolina.

Wild and domesticated animals supplied a variety of meat and dairy products for the colonials. Deer and small game were especially plentiful. Large stocks of cattle provided beef for the colonial table. Hogs thrived to the extent that pork--salted or on the hoof--was one of the colony's principal items of export and earned the Carolinians the nickname "porkers." The colonials tended to let the cattle and hogs forage for themselves in the woods, however, thereby reducing the quality of meat derived from the animals. Most families also kept a number of sheep though primarily for wool; North Carolinians were not as fond of mutton as their English counterparts. Goats were raised sparingly because they were not worth the trouble. Such animals played havoc with crops and gardens.

Domestic fowl added another dimension to the colonial diet. Geese, ducks, turkeys, and chickens abounded around the houses and barns. Feathers as well as meat and poultry products rendered these "dunghill fowl" valuable. Despite a favorable climate and an abundance of food, particularly corn, only a small percentage of barnyard fowl lived to maturity due to the mismanagement or neglect of the colonials. Still, North Carolina planters took pride in their reputation, whether true or not, of having the largest flocks of domestic poultry in the British empire.

Pork was a staple food of the colonial Carolinians. "Pig scalding" was a necessary part of the preparation and often done in the primitive fashion shown here. From Benjamin Butterworth (arranger and compiler), *The Growth of Industrial Art* (Washington: Government Printing Office, 1892).

Along the coast and rivers the people supplemented their diets with varieties of sea life. Seafoods, particularly oysters, were a staple in the meals of Beaufort residents. The provincials often fished in the inland waters, more for food than for pleasure. Travelers, commenting on the swarming of the rock bass at the falls of the Roanoke River near Halifax, said that a dog thrown into the water would not be able to swim to the other side due to the congestion of fish. This phenomenon was called the "rock fight," and men easily killed the fish with sticks. On the Roanoke and other rivers mullet, trout, and perch prompted fishermen to stretch weirs or nets across the water to catch the fish. These nets so greatly interfered with navigation that the provincial assembly passed legislation to regulate that type of fishing activity.

Most colonials, rich and poor alike, maintained orchards from which they derived fruit and liquor. The principal fruits were apples and peaches from which huge quantities of brandy and cider were made. These fruits were so abundant that travelers passing by an apple or peach orchard felt free to help themselves to the fruit, and the owners were not only unoffended but encouraged such license since the fruit was so plentiful that it was rarely sold. In fact, during season the colonials even fed apples and peaches to their hogs. Less common fruits included pears, apricots, cherries, quinces, and plums.

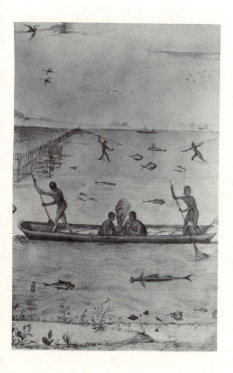

Colonials and Indians alike used weirs and nets for catching fish. A weir was actually a fence constructed in a stream or waterway. Such a device is pictured in Paul Hulton and David Beers Quinn, *The American Drawings of John White, 1577-1590* (Chapel Hill: University of North Carolina Press, 1964), II, Plate 42.

The drinking habits of Carolinians clearly indicated a propensity for alcoholic beverages. The colonials imported wines, rum, and malt liquors; they manufactured whiskey, brandy, and cider. During the colonial era distilling became a major industry in the province. However, only a minority of the people owned stills because the apparatus was very expensive. Such property was carefully preserved and bequeathed at a man's death to his wife or children that they might "still" their own liquor. The possession of less expensive apple mills was more widespread.

The consumption of liquor was not reserved for any age, sex, or class. Infants might drink cider and three-year-old children a glass of rum in the mornings to ward off "noxious vapors." Delicate women downed hard cider. And the colonials drank on every possible occasion. Weddings, funerals, ordinations, vestry meetings, musters, elections, court meetings, slave auctions, and house-raisings occasioned the outpouring of spirits. Such activities as musters and house-raisings were often subverted by the consumption of excessive quantities of rum or brandy.

The origin as well as variety of drinks provides additional information about colonial liquors. Madeira seemed the most popular wine followed by claret and red ports, probably from Great Britain. Wines were also imported from Teneriffe Island in the Canaries and the southern European countries. Rum came from the New England colonies and the West Indies. William Byrd found the rum from New England so bad that it was aptly called "Kill-Devil," a universal terminology applied to rum drink in seventeenth century America. Imported beer originated primarily in Philadelphia and New York but occasionally arrived from Bristol in England. A variety of homemade beer was that derived from persimmons. Where apples and peaches were scarce, Carolinians picked ripe persimmons, combined them with wheat bran, and kneaded the mixture into loaves which were baked in ovens. From these was brewed a fermented liquor called persimmon beer which had an acceptable taste. The colonials produced most of their brandy and cider in North Carolina though French brandy was relished when it could be obtained. Occasionally brandy was distilled from potatoes which produced a much less desirable drink.

Of course the colonials mixed their drinks. Flips were warm drinks containing mostly strong beer sweetened with sugar or molasses and flavored with a "touch" of rum. Punches were a universal and potent mixture of tea, rum (arrack), sugar, lemons (or lemon juice, limes, or oranges), and water. Grog contained water with a fourth, fifth, or sixth part of rum. Toddies usually included rum, water, and sugar though occasionally brandy was substituted for the rum. Bumbo consisted of half rum and half water with sugar added. Wines as well as rum admitted of mixture. Wine, sugar, water, and a little nutmeg produced sangaree; wine, sugar, and fresh milk yielded syllabub.

Trade with foreign nations
brought into the colonies a variety of coins such as this
Spanish milled dollar from the
museum's collection. Both sides
of the coin are pictured above,
and the date 1770 is quite clear.
Photographed by Charles A. Clark,
Division of Archives and History,
for use in the *North Carolina
Historical Review* (Summer, 1973),
239.

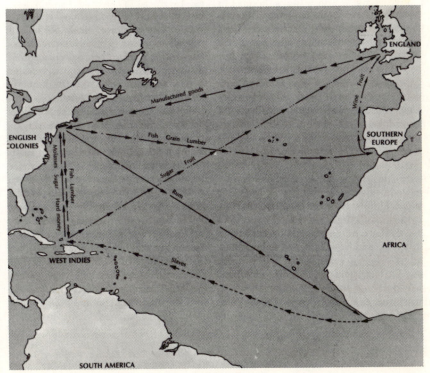

The patterns of popular trade routes ca. 1650 are traced on this map from
Oscar Theodore Barck and Hugh Talmage Lefler, *A History of the United States*,
2 volumes (New York: Ronald Press Company, 1968), I, 78.

Carolinians were not totally addicted to alcoholic beverages, however. They consumed large amounts of coffee, tea, and chocolate, particularly for breakfast. The colonials, being largely Britishers, drank much tea which they imported, sometimes legally from Great Britain but often smuggled from Holland. They also concocted their own brand of the drink from the Yaupon bush or tree, a variety of the southern holly. This must have complemented the smuggled Dutch tea especially well after the colonials agreed not to import tea from Britain in protest against the Townshend tea tax in 1767.

Meals varied according to the economic fortunes of the people. Among the wealthy they constituted one of the daily burdens of the mistress of the house who directed the activities of the household. It was she who supervised the poultry yard, dairy, and smokehouse, and it was she who determined the variety of dishes prepared for the meals. Of course she was aided by a bevy of servants and guided in the preparation of dishes by directions from mother, advice of friends, and written treatises such as E. Smith's *The Compleat Housewife* and Martha Bradley's *The British Housewife*. Resulting dishes were often rich, well-seasoned, and complicated. Tables fairly groaned under the offerings of meats, vegetables, pastries, and beverages. The always bountiful table of William Dry caused his residence just north of Brunswick to be known as the house of universal hospitality.

The meals of the wealthy were leisurely, luxurious affairs, The men of the gentry rose late in the morning and breakfasted between nine and ten o'clock on cold meats, fowl, hominy, bread and butter, and tea or coffee. Dinner, between two o'clock and four-thirty, constituted the principal meal of the day. One traveler reported being dined on fat roasted turkeys, geese, ducks, boiled fowls, large hams, hung beef, and barbecued pig. Vegetables and such pastries as minced pies, cheesecakes, tarts, and biscuits supplemented that repast. Gentlemen drank ciders, toddies, punches, and particularly wines. Toasts were profuse, as many as twenty to thirty being offered at a single meal. After a late afternoon tea, a light supper was eaten between eight and ten o'clock.

The lower-and middle-class individuals might rise about six in the morning, have a strong drink, work for two or three hours, and breakfast at nine or ten o'clock on a variety of cold meats, hominy, toast, bread and butter, tea, coffee, or chocolate, and cider. Dinner, enjoyed in mid-afternoon, consisted of the standing dishes of ham, pork, and greens, plus cider or brandy. Often these people omitted supper, instead sipping some alcoholic drink during the late evening.

The fare was not always desirable. The journey of William Logan through North Carolina in 1745 found him eating at one Chilly's house between Edenton and Bath where he had "some chickens broiled in a nasty manner" for his dinner. Before he reached New Bern he stopped at a house where he was "vilely entertained, having nothing but Potato Bread mixed with Indian Corn & rank Irish Butter. . . ."

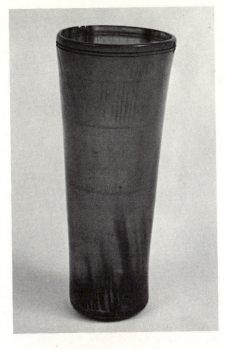

Animal horns were used to make useful articles such as this cup which is in the museum's collection. It is 5 1/2 inches high, has a top diameter of 2 1/2 inches, and a base diameter of 1 1/2 inches. Photograph was executed by Charles A. Clark, Division of Archives and History, for use in the *North Carolina Historical Review* (Summer, 1973), 245.

And about fifteen miles north of Wilmington Logan stopped at another house where the inhabitants had been subsisting for days on potatoes and some chickens. On the other hand, a French traveler in 1765 dined at a farmer's home on good fat bacon, greens, corn bread, and fine cider.

The diet of the slaves was scanty and unwholesome. Upon rising at daybreak they received a small amount of hominy or hoecake and then worked until noon. At that time they might receive an hour's respite during which they ate dinner of hominy with salt, perhaps flavored once or twice a week with a little fat, skimmed milk, bacon, or salt fish. After dusk, if work lasted that long, the slaves consumed their last meal of the day, generally consisting of the same monotonous corn products. The more fortunate plantation slaves were permitted small gardens which they tended in their spare moments on weekdays and on Sundays. The produce either supplemented their diets or was sold or exchanged for articles of clothing, pipes, and knives.

Candles and lamps provided illumination for the meals and other household activities. Tallow made from every type of fat and grease was saved for candles. Wax candles were less common though most farmers kept several hives of bees from which they derived wax as well as honey. Few Carolinians availed themselves of the berries of the myrtle which grew profusely along the coast. Plucking and boiling the berries several times for a few hours would have yielded excellent wax but the people shied from the work involved.

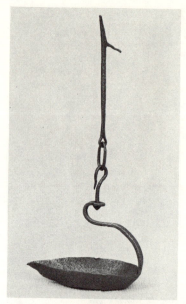

Lanterns and Betty lamps provided inexpensive light for colonials. The Betty lamp was filled with tallow, grease, or oil in which a rag or wick was soaked and then ignited. The flame produced had an offensive odor. The lantern, with its horn-covered opening, could be used outside and was no doubt an indispensable item for the traveler. Both artifacts are in the museum's collection and were photographed by Charles A. Clark, Division of Archives and History, for use in the *North Carolina Historical Review* (Summer, 1973), 234.

Lamps were a rarer form of illumination. The earliest were various forms of fat lamps; the most popular were the Betty lamps which were small, shallow receptacles with projecting noses. They were filled with tallow, grease, or oil and a piece of rag or coarse wick was laid on the nose. From the Betty lamps came a "dull, smoky, ill-smelling flame." Between 1785 and 1800 Betty lamps were succeeded by more sophisticated pewter and glass lamps of various shapes and sizes.

In addition to candlemaking, another household manufacture was reflected in the numerous spinning wheels found in the colonial homes. Most households contained at least one linen wheel and one woolen wheel plus sets of cards used for straightening cotton and wool fibers. After carding, the fibers were spun into thread, which was used for weaving the family's cloth. Many colonials, however, depended upon weavers, tailors, or friends with looms to weave the thread into their "country-made" cloth. Bulky, expensive, and complicated looms were not standard items in the households though they appeared more frequently towards the close of the colonial period. Girls were taught to knit at an early age, and knitted apparel formed an integral part of the family clothing.

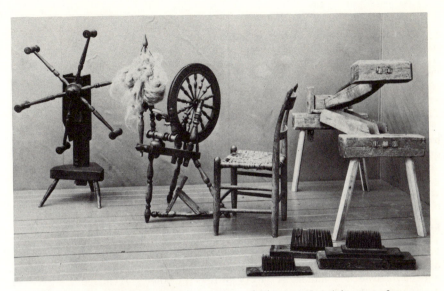

Visitors to the North Carolina Museum of History, Raleigh, are often invited to watch demonstrations of spinning and weaving on the various colonial devices which are displayed in the museum. Photograph from the files of the Division of Archives and History.

The colonials were far from self-sufficient when clothing themselves. Tailor-made garments and finished articles of clothing sold by merchants were exceedingly popular. Since clothing often represented a considerable investment, the colonials selected their wardrobes carefully. The fabrics used in making clothes varied widely. Irish linen, particularly checked linen, always found a ready market. Holland, a glazed or unglazed cotton or linen, sold well. The most popular material was probably Osnabrig (Osnaburg), a coarse linen originally made in Osnabruck, Germany. Still, the list would not be complete without mentioning Belgian duffil (duffel), German serge, French lawn and cambric, Oriental calico, muslin, and Persian as well as fearnought, drugget, shalloon, frieze, chintz, buckram, durance, and dowlas among many other materials.

Various types of clothing characterized colonial dress. For women the outermost garment was a gown probably composed of a skirt, bodice, and sleeves which tied or buttoned to the bodice. One or more petticoats, sometimes designated as "top" and "under" petticoats, were worn under the gown, beneath which a loose linen shift served as the essential item of underclothing. To prevent undue soiling of the skirts, aprons were commonly worn. Neckcloths served a similar purpose for the bodice. Footwear included thread, silk, or worsted stockings, and leather, cloth, or silk shoes, sometimes accompanied by clogs, or half-slippers with wooden soles, to protect the shoes from mud and water. Caps, bonnets, and hats covered the head, while cloaks and hoods gave added warmth in cool weather. Gloves, often kid, were popular; handkerchiefs abounded.

The wardrobe of Mary Gainor of Edgecombe County might illustrate the clothing of a North Carolina woman in the colonial era. She owned eleven gowns, five petticoats, five shifts, two hats, two pairs of gloves, two pairs of stockings, one pair of shoes, and a "parcel" of caps, handkerchiefs, and aprons. The wife of justice of the peace Jesse Hare possessed ten gowns, nine petticoats, three riding coats, two cloaks, two fine aprons, two fine handkerchiefs, five caps, one hat, one pair of hose, and two pairs of shoes. These women and others enhanced their inherent beauty with rings, bracelets, necklaces, lockets, earrings, and other jewelry. The daughter of Gov. Gabriel Johnston owned five gold lockets, a garnet necklace set in silver, a Bristol stone necklace set in silver, a gold watch and chain, a set of gold tweezers, a gold girdle buckle, and a Bristol stone girdle buckle set in silver.

William Gainor, husband of Mary, displayed an average variety and amount of clothing for a man. He possessed one coat, three jackets, three pairs of breeches, two shirts, one hat, and two caps. Vests and waistcoats were also common items of male attire, accompanied by coats and "greatcoats" when added protection or warmth was needed. Breeches ended slightly below the knee, although long breeches or trousers were not uncommon. Many planters found leather breeches desirable because of their durability. Silk, worsted, or thread stockings supported by garters covered the calf of the leg. Shoes and boots formed the preponderance of footwear, but pumps occasionally appeared.

Caps, including nightcaps, were widely worn. Most men also owned at least one or two hats, which were generally made of felt or beaver. However, other furs, more expensive than beaver, were used for hatmaking. Constant Devotion, a hatter, left at his death not only 28 beaver skins and 33 beaver hats but also 155 raccoon skins, 4 otter skins, and 5 muskrat skins.

Hannah Iredell (Mrs. James Iredell), of Edenton, wore this dress when she attended a reception in Philadelphia given in honor of George Washington. Made of imported green silk with an ecru organdy fichu and petticoat, the dress shows the French influence on style in the 1770s. This garment was restored by Mr. Pete Ballard of Winston-Salem.

Men also had many opportunities to display jewelry. Silver knee and shoe buckles were common. So were silver breeches buckles and clasps as well as ivory and gilt vest buttons. Rings, gold and silver, were popular, particularly mourning rings which were given by the family of a deceased person to close friends and relatives. Snuffboxes, elaborately adorned, and watches added glamour to the male attire.

Fashion-conscious women and men attempted to stay abreast of the latest styles of hair dress. The advertisement of James Verrier, peruke and hatmaker in New Bern, announced that he dressed

> ladies and gentlemen's hair in the newest and best approved fashion and [made] all sorts of ladies full dress toupees, [undress] toupees, plain rolls, beads pleats, and side curls, convenient for dress and undress, also all sorts of gentlemen's full dress bag and bob wigs, . . . false tails and curls, likewise spring curls for gentlemen whose side locks are thin or come off, so natural as not to be discovered by the most curious eye.

Wigs remained popular throughout the colonial era, but toward the approach of the Revolution a preference for natural hair became evident.

Clothing for children closely resembled that of adults. Of course the wearing apparel varied according to age and wealth. The more fortunate--that is, wealthy--boys received from two to five shirts a year, one or two pairs of breeches or trousers, perhaps a matching waistcoat and breeches, and probably a coat or jacket. Rapid growth of children necessitated at least one pair of shoes per year which was often supplemented by a pair of boots. Occasionally a pair of yarn stockings accompanied the acquisition of shoes. The boys expected one hat per year, usually felt or beaver but sometimes raccoon.

Buckles, besides being utilitarian, were also ornamental. The knee buckle shown at the left once belonged to Kenneth Black of Moore County, who was a friend of Flora MacDonald. The silver snuffbox pictured in the upper photograph reputedly belonged to Thomas Burke, colonial governor of North Carolina, 1781-1782. Both items were photographed by Charles A. Clark and are in the museum's collection.

The amount of clothing acquired yearly by girls has been more difficult to determine. Often cloth was purchased for the girls, as much as thirty yards a year, which the girls, their families, or tailors converted into finished items of clothing such as gowns, petticoats, sacks, shifts, banyons, and jackets. The girls received at least one pair of shoes and stockings annually in addition to a pair of gloves and handkerchiefs. Caps and hats were also standard attire.

The clothing of the slaves was minimal. Young children often ran about naked, while even the older slaves in some instances wore only a breechclout or petticoat. Nevertheless, records show that many masters afforded slaves better treatment. Ben and Chloe, two young slaves who belonged to an orphan in Edgecombe County, received excellent care from the orphan's guardian. Both were usually given a pair of shoes and a blanket each year; in addition Ben annually received pants, coat, and a jacket, and Chloe a shift and jacket. Advertisements for runaway slaves also indicated that they were well clothed. Richmond, who belonged to the company of Ancrum and Schaw in Wilmington, wore a white shirt, leather breeches, striped flannel jacket, and a pair of shoes and stockings at his departure. Many others were similarly clad in a diverse selection of clothes.

Despite the variety and even elegance of clothes, North Carolinians apparently took poor care of them. A traveler in the Cape Fear area in the 1770s found the people to be among the worst "clothes washers" that she had ever seen. All clothes, regardless of material or color, were thrown together in a copper or iron pot with boiling water and a piece of soap. After being turned over a few times with a stick, the clothes were removed, rinsed, squeezed, and put on pales to dry. Bleaching was disregarded. The same observer also noted that Cape Fear housewives shunned soap-making. Although the quality of potash in the area was excellent, the women preferred to purchase soap at extravagant prices. And then they often received inferior Irish soap.

The colonials owned a myriad of personal items to bring a measure of comfort, convenience, and safety into their lives. A smooth face demanded a razor, hone, and looking glass; neatness necessitated hatbrushes, clothesbrushes, and shoebrushes. Poor vision accounted for numerous pairs of spectacles. The minuteman

Weapons of all kinds were valued by colonial men. The harquebus pictured at the left was a heavy matchlock or wheel-lock gun of a type dating from the 1400s. The sword depicted at the right dates from the period of Charles II. Both articles are in the museum's collection and were photographed by Charles A. Clark for use in the *North Carolina Historical Review* (Summer, 1973), 237.

concept of every colonial male ready to spring armed to a call of distress hardly applied to the North Carolinians. Perhaps two thirds of the men kept guns--pistols, double-barreled pistols, muskets, rifles, shotguns, and blunderbusses. Such accouterments as powderhorns, shot bags, shot, powder, flints, and cartouche boxes accompanied the guns. As many as one fifth of the colonials also owned swords or cutlasses. Clocks, chamber pots, and mousetraps might indicate the diversity of other articles in the households.

Men often brought the tools of their occupation to their houses, or perhaps to separate rooms or wings adjoining the buildings. The workbench of Thomas Hobgood, turner and joiner, contained one tenant saw, one handsaw, four gouges, two files, two augers, nine chisels, one cooper's adze, four planes, one froe, two drawing knives, one shaving knife, four plane irons, one hammer, one taper bit, one gimlet, one mandrel, one compass, one ruler, one jointer, some brass nails, a glue pot, and "some other tools." Shoemakers, hatters, and physicians also worked inside. Furthermore, men who were primarily planters generally kept a variety of tools, such as those of carpentry and shoemaking, needed for making the simple articles required by a family.

The clutter outside the house under sheds or lean-tos and in barns or small outbuildings was as great as that found inside. Saddles, bridles, and halters hung from the walls as did reaphooks, scythes, and pieces of rope. Horse collars and hames awaited use, while various tubs, pails, baskets, and casks occupied much space. Every man possessed an ax and hatchet in addition to a pair of iron wedges for splitting wood. Steelyards for weighing agricultural produce were a vital part of the household. Tools and implements such as hoes, plows, flails, and brakes reflected the cultivation of tobacco, corn, cotton, flax, wheat, and rice among other crops. (Two other pamphlets in this series describe the development of agriculture in North Carolina: Cornelius O. Cathey, *Agriculture in North Carolina Before the Civil War*; and Jerome E. Brooks, *Green Leaf and Gold: Tobacco in North Carolina*.)

Two necessary tools for colonial builders were the adze shown at the left and the froe pictured at the right. The adze was used in dressing timber and the froe was used in splitting logs. The inset shows the manner of riving clapboards from a log. Photographs, used by permission, are from *Colonial Living* by Edwin Tunis, copyright (c) 1957; published by William Collins+World Publishing Company.

To amplify this general description of the colonial household a discussion of a few selected areas of colonial social history will serve to represent the richness and variety of the provincial life-style. The topics include education, recreation, health, marriage, and death.

This collection of agricultural tools used by North Carolina settlers was preserved by the Wachovia Historical Society, Old Salem, and pictured in Arnett, *The Story of North Carolina*, 154. Implements include: (1) vegetable chopper; (2) iron rake; (3) iron pitchfork; (4) wooden pitchfork; (5) sickle; (6) flail; (7) tomahawk; (8) hackles; (9) root-grubber; (10) weight; (11) sausage-mill; (12) pick; (13) swingle; (14) hackle cover; (15) flax break.

Education in terms of institutionalized instruction was closely allied with the Anglican church. The first known schoolteacher in the colony was Charles Griffin, a lay reader of the Anglican church who came from the West Indies in 1705 to open a school in Pasquotank County near Nixonton. Griffin departed the colony in 1709, ultimately to teach at the College of William and Mary, and was succeeded by the Reverend James Adams. By 1712 a Mr. Mashburn had opened another church-related school in Chowan County near Sarum on the Virginia border which was so highly regarded that families many miles distant sent their children for instruction.

As settlement expanded, so did the number of schools. Anglican missionary James Moir taught in Brunswick in 1745, and the Reverend Alexander Stuart established a school in Hyde County in 1763. The Reverend Daniel Earl, rector of St. Paul's Parish in Chowan, opened a school at his home on the Chowan River about fifteen miles from Edenton in the 1750s. Assisted by his daughter Nancy, Earl not only offered his students formal disciplinary study but also instructed the people of the area in the cultivation of flax, methods of weaving, and even the art of shad-and-herring-fishing, which earned him the nickname of the "Herring-catching Parson."

The most notable institution of education affiliated with the Anglican church was the academy established in New Bern in 1764. The Reverend James Reed initiated the school in conjunction with a number of public-spirited citizens of New Bern and Craven County. Although the academy was supported primarily by a tax on imported liquors and legislative appropriations, the school was intended by its founders as a church school, remaining under the control of the church and exercising a religious influence on its pupils.

Thomas Tomlinson, who had emigrated from England at the instance of his brother who lived near New Bern, taught the school. From 1764 until his departure for Rhode Island in 1772 Tomlinson proved a capable teacher. However, he was faced with disciplinary problems. American parents excessively indulged their children, and this condition was exacerbated by the coeducational character of the New Bern academy. Tomlinson eventually incurred the enmity of two of the trustees of the school when he disciplined and expelled their children. Thereafter, one of the trustees sought to undermine the institution by curtailing its enrollment and stopping payment of Tomlinson's salary. Eventually Tomlinson was dismissed.

A similar academy was established in Edenton. The legislature had authorized a school in the town in 1745 but not until the 1760s, when citizens of Edenton by a voluntary cooperative effort erected a schoolhouse, did the school materialize. Legislation in 1770 confirmed the institution and provided monetary support for it.

Three typical log houses are pictured on this page. Above, at left, is the cabin reputed to have been the first house in Salem. Built in January, 1766, it fell in January, 1907. (Original photograph was the property of the late Adelaide L. Fries and was pictured in Arnett, *The Story of North Carolina*, 162.) Above, at right, is the Sanders log cabin, located at Southern Pines in Moore County; and at lower left is the Allen House, located at the Alamance Battleground State Historic Site in Alamance County. Pictures of the Sanders House and the Allen House from the files of the Survey Unit, Division of Archives and History.

The immigration of Scotch-Irish and Germans stimulated education in the colony. In 1760 the Reverend James Tate, a Presbyterian, opened the first classical academy in colonial North Carolina in Wilmington. The most famous academy in the province was that of the Reverend David Caldwell, a graduate of Princeton College and a Presbyterian minister. Caldwell started his "Log College" in 1767 near Greensboro, and enrolled fifty to sixty students each year. For forty years he trained future physicians, ministers, lawyers, judges, governors, and congressmen of the colony and the state.

The Moravians gave careful attention to the education of their children, though the first settlements did not include enough young people to justify formal educational institutions. In 1762 separate schools were established in Bathabara for the boys and girls of the town. About the same time a school was opened in Bathania which was three miles from Bathabara, and in 1771 the little community of Friedburg offered instruction to its youth. The next year a girls' school opened in Salem followed in 1774 by a boys' school. Generally, the education provided by the Moravian schools did not continue beyond the fundamentals of reading, writing, and arithmetic, though a few boys and girls pursued their studies to enter academies in Pennsylvania.

Many nonsectarian public and private schools offered educational opportunities to the youth of North Carolina. The schools might be sponsored by a wealthy individual, initiated by an organized effort on the part of neighboring families, or instigated by an aspiring teacher. At least two individuals provided endowments in their wills for free schools. By his will in 1744 James Winwright of Carteret County appropriated all the rents and profits of his lands and houses in Beaufort for the hiring of a schoolmaster to teach reading, writing, and arithmetic to children of the area. Money was also set aside for the construction of a school and house for the master. The results of the Winwright gift are not known, but within five years of its donation there was a schoolhouse at the Straits, not far from Beaufort. In 1765 the vestry of St. John's Parish in Carteret County appointed a man to employ three schoolteachers to serve the parish. Col. James Innes of New Hanover County by his will in 1760 set aside money for a free school for "the benefit of the youth of North Carolina," but his legacy was not utilized until after the Revolution.

When free or private schools were unavailable, children received instruction from parents, older brothers and sisters, tutors, and itinerant schoolmasters; and North Carolinians were concerned about the education of their children. Many stipulated in their wills that their children, grandchildren, nieces, and nephews should be educated in the best manner possible. Mary Conway wanted her son schooled in such a fashion as to qualify him "for such business or profession as his Genius shall most incline to." Edward Moseley recommended that one of his sons be trained in the law, "it being highly necessary in so Large a Family. . . ."

The children of the poor and orphans were not neglected. In addition to the free schools envisioned by Winwright, Innes, and possibly others, numerous legacies were left to the poor. John Bennett of Currituck County bequeathed forty shillings to educate two poor children for one year. Orphans with sufficient estates were placed with guardians who would educate and provide for the children "according to their Rank & degree." Otherwise the orphans were apprenticed to learn a handicraft or trade and at the same time to read and write.

The quality of instruction which was offered the children varied greatly. Anglican ministers such as the Reverend Thomas Burgess of Halifax County usually possessed an extensive educational background. However, in Edgecombe County Thomas Bell augmented his carpenter's income with a teaching supplement, while Henry Tanton resorted to the classroom when old age and infirmities prevented him from active physical work. Janet Schaw stated that in the Wilmington area one of John Rutherfurd's sons hated his schoolmaster because the teacher knew so much less than the student.

The early schools in the colonial era were vague imitations of the Latin grammar schools in England. They provided a narrow curriculum which emphasized the classics and was designed to prepare students for college. Late in the colonial period, academies, the forerunners of modern high schools and the distributors of education to the majority who would not go to college, became popular. Newspaper advertisements by schoolmasters also indicated an increasing concern for a practical education which became characteristic of the American educational process. Elias Hoell in 1774 offered Craven County residents two classes of study: reading, writing, ciphering, navigation, and surveying; and algebra, Euclid's *Elements*, Latin, and Greek. The next year Florence McCarthy, teacher of mathematics and the English language, opened an academy in New Bern where he taught English grammar, writing, arithmetic, Italian bookkeeping, navigation, gauging, algebra, geometry, trigonometry, surveying, and other subjects.

Education, of course, was more inclusive than a formal course of study from textbooks. Wyriot Ormond in 1773 warned his executors that no expense was too great for the education of his two daughters and added, "I not only mean that part of their Education which Respects their Schooling, but Every Other that Can be had for their Advantage." Gov. Gabriel Johnston elaborated on this point in his will in 1751 when he stated that

> I Earnestly Request my Dearest Wife be a kind tender Mother to my Dear little Girl, and to bring her up in the Fear of God and under a deep Sense of her being always in his Presence, and in Sobriety and Moderation Confining her Desires to things Plain, neat and Elegant, and not aspiring after the Gayety, Splendor and Extravagances; and Especially, to take Care to keep within the Bounds of her Incomes, and by no Means to Run in Debt.

Higher education of necessity was obtained outside the colony. The wealthy sent their children to Virginia, Pennsylvania, New Jersey, New England, and occasionally to Scotland and England to finish their schooling. Edward Moseley made provision for the education of his children after they had exhausted the resources of the "Common Masters" in North Carolina. Cullen Pollock instructed that his sons, after learning as much as possible in North Carolina, be sent to Boston for further education and remain there in the care of some prudent person until they reached the age of eighteen. John Pfifer of Mecklenburg County left funds for the education of his children, particularly his son Paul who was to "be put through a liberal Education and Colleged."

The college made a tardy appearance in North Carolina. The first effort to establish a college was made in 1754 when the legislature provided funds for an institution to "promote good order, Literature, and true Religion, in all parts of this province." Unfortunately the French and Indian War proved so costly that the college moneys were used for military purposes.

The idea of establishing a college was revived by Presbyterian residents of Mecklenburg County who persuaded Gov. William Tryon to recommend to the assembly the erection of a seminary in the backcountry. The assembly agreed and passed legislation in 1771 entitled "An Act for establishing and endowing of Queen's College in the Town of Charlotte in Mecklenburg County." The legislation pointed out the need for "a Seminary of Learning" for students who had obtained sufficient knowledge of Latin, Greek, and Hebrew, and who could acquire the principles of "Science and Virtue" which would make them better citizens of their communities. Public tax moneys and private donations would support the institution.

The law stated that the president had to belong to the Established Church, but it did not specify that the "three or less tutors" had to be licensed by either the Bishop of London or by the governor. Although Governor Tryon assented to the measure, the crown then disallowed the law in 1772. North Carolinians did not learn of that action until 1773, and by that time the college had already opened. It continued to operate under the name of Queen's Museum without the benefit of legislative approval or public tax support. In 1777 it was rechartered under the name Liberty Hall Academy.

The new state constitution of 1776 envisioned the founding of one or more state-supported universities. Between 1776 and 1789 a large number of academies which served as high schools were chartered by the assembly in an attempt to prepare students for college study. Liberty Hall in Charlotte was one of those academies. After the turmoil of the Revolutionary years had abated, North Carolina became one of the first states to propose the establishment of a university funded by the state.

Education in a broader sense encompassed more than academic instruction. The extent and nature of the Carolinians' collections of books reflected their educational attainments as well as cultural concerns. Records indicate that at least two thirds of the colonials owned books. Many possessed only a Bible. Most had five or more books, and some amassed large private libraries. The Reverend James Reed owned 266 volumes; Dr. John Eustace, 282; Edward Mosely, 400; James Milner, 621; and Samuel Johnston, over 1,000 in a collection started by his uncle, Governor Johnston. The subjects of most of the books would be encompassed under the headings of theology, moral philosophy, literature, history, law, and medicine. They were often written in Latin, Greek, Hebrew, and French, as well as in English.

Recreation

For the provincials in North Carolina recreation served not only as a respite from work but also as a means of socializing. Men gathered for log-rollings, house-raisings, and corn-shuckings, while women engaged in quilting bees and spinning matches. Less productive activities such as jumping, wrestling, and quoits, a game similar to horseshoes, occupied the males at public gatherings.

Dancing was a popular pastime, particularly when fiddles or bagpipes could be obtained for accompaniment. However, musical instruments were scarce and often Carolinians were forced to resort to singing in the absence of instrumental music. The most popular instrument was the fiddle or violin. A study of Edgecombe County before the Revolution also revealed the presence of horns and drums in the homes, and six Jew's harps on the shelves of merchant Robert Hilliard.

The Moravians provided an exception to the dearth of instrumental music in the province. Music was an integral part of their lives and particularly of their religious services. The first immigrants brought a "horn" with them and three months later opened an evening service with a new trumpet which they had made from a hollow tree. By 1755 French horns and flutes appeared in Bethabara, violins in 1756, a small organ in 1762, and a set of trombones in 1768. Gov. William Tryon's wife, who visited Wachovia with her husband in 1767, enjoyed playing the organ. Still, it should be remembered that the Moravians utilized their music primarily for religious purposes rather than for recreation.

The colonials also appreciated the more formal dances. Lawyer Waightstill Avery participated in a "splendid Ball" one evening in 1769 in the town of Halifax. When James Milner was selected to represent Tarboro in the provincial assembly in 1772, he gave an elegant supper for the leading gentlemen of the town and Edgecombe County after which there was a ball "which was greatly embellished by a very numerous and brilliant Appearance of most charming Ladies. . . ." Indeed Milner was so greatly admired that the following epigram was concocted:

May Milner's name in future Annals shine,
And Edgecombe's grateful Sons approve each Line
May future Patriots aim, like him, to be
Renown'd for Honor and Integrity;
And may the Nine, in their harmonious Lays,
Attest his Merit and record his Praise.

And in 1775 Wilmingtonians hastened to conduct another ball before such frivolous activities were banned by the local Committee of Safety as unbecoming for patriots engaged in a struggle for their liberty.

North Carolinians seemed excessively fond of gaming, especially dice, cards, billiards, bowls, chess, checkers, and backgammon. Among the various card games enjoyed by the men were whist, the forerunner of bridge, piquet, quadrille, and all-fours. The arrival of three ships from London at the close of the colonial era carrying 154, 576, and 888 packs of cards respectively indicated the popularity of that form of entertainment.

Moreover, every newcomer to North Carolina underwent a "seasoning process" by which immigrants were acclimated to the province. Often the process was fatal. If not it rarely bestowed total immunity. Those who settled in the low, swampy areas of the eastern portions of the colony suffered most. The fevers and agues were particularly acute in the autumn months, and as many as nine people were buried in one day in Edenton alone. The "sickly season" was not always confined to the coastal region. The Moravians also suffered each fall and spring from similar illnesses which only cold weather could terminate. Some residents of the colony, including Governor Tryon, appreciated the therapeutic effects of the coastal air and water, and sent their families to the seashore to recover their health.

Mortality was greatest among infants and children. The experience of the Anglican congregation in St. Philip's Parish, Charleston, South Carolina, was probably representative of North Carolina. In St. Philip's Parish in 1756, thirty-five of 105 recorded deaths were those of children under three years of age. Still, some colonials lived to old ages. In 1772 six men in Carteret County petitioned for exemption from public taxes because of their advanced ages. One was sixty, three over sixty, one seventy, and one ninety. Then, of course, the elderly were afflicted with diseases peculiar to old age such as heart conditions and nephritis, which was termed fits, dropsy, and decay.

In eighteenth century England the medical profession consisted of physicians, surgeons, and apothecaries. Physicians were the elite of the medical profession. They usually held university degrees, practiced largely among the upper class, were "internists," and enjoyed the title "doctor" whatever the degree. Surgeons received training by apprenticeship and hospital work, worked chiefly on external problems, and were addressed as "mister." Apothecaries also lacked the elevated status of physicians; they sold and sometimes prescribed drugs.

In the colonies the above distinctions were blurred. Most of the doctors were surgeon apothecaries rather than the distinguished scholarly gentlemen physicians. They merely assumed the title of doctor. There seemed to be no lack of surgeon apothecaries or "doctors" in the more populous regions of the provinces. Throughout the colonies the ratio of doctors to population approximated one to 600; and in the urban areas, for example New York in 1750, the ratio dropped to one to 350. In Wilmington, North Carolina, at least twenty-four doctors practiced before 1778 which in any given year would probably have provided the town with a better ratio than the New York figure. Among the Wilmington practitioners were Armand John DeRosset and Moses John DeRosset, father and son. An affinity for physicians was shown by Rebecca Green, daughter of Dr. Samuel Green, who married first Dr. John Mortimer and upon his death, Dr. James Geekie.

The Moravians provided Piedmont settlers with several well-trained physicians. Dr. Hans Martin Kalberlahn served Wachovia and the surrounding area from 1753 to 1759 when he died in a typhus epidemic. Patients came to Dr. Kalberlahn from as far away as 100 miles. He successfully completed several operations including trepanning (removing a piece of cranial bone) the head of a man who had been struck by an ax. A Dr. Schubert and Dr. Jacob Bonn succeeded Dr. Kalberlahn in the Piedmont.

Doctors, like many other creditors in North Carolina, found payment for their services slow and small. As Alexander Pope said:

> God and the Doctor we alike adore,
> But only when in danger, not before;
> The danger over, both are alike requited,
> God is forgotten and the Doctor slighted.

In some areas of North Carolina if a patient thought a practitioner's fee was too high, it was customary to submit the matter to another doctor or doctors who might approve the fee or reduce the charge according to the friendliness of their relationship with their colleague.

Marriage

Contemporary evidence suggests that Carolinians, particularly the women, married at young ages and raised large families. On the frontier women offered companionship for the men, and children provided the necessary labor force on the farms. Edenton physician John Brickell stated that a girl was "reckoned a stale maid" if she remained unmarried at twenty years of age, and that women in North Carolina were very fruitful, most houses being full of little ones. Although the average number of children in the colonial family cannot be precisely determined, one systematic study found an average of four children per family. Many families, however, were much larger.

Weddings tended to be happy though not riotous social occasions. Before 1766 only Anglican ministers, or in their absence, justices of the peace, could perform marriage ceremonies. The scarcity of Anglican clergymen placed the burden of marriage services upon the justices and caused many of the ceremonies to be private affairs. Since women lost title of their property to their husbands when they married, some females chose to protect their holdings by marriage settlements, which reserved property to the wives or directed the disposal of the property at their deaths. Divorce was not legal, but courts occasionally sanctioned separations in cases of desertion or adultery as long as the wife and children were adequately supported. Joseph and Mary McGehe of Bute County announced via a newspaper advertisement in 1775 that they had agreed upon a permanent separation whereby both considered their marriage terminated.

Death in the colonial period occasioned great sorrow among family and friends as it does today. Of course, death was more frequent and life expectancy shorter due to ignorance of personal hygiene, more primitive medicines, and less advanced medical practices. This did not mean that personal grief was less intense but that people were more accustomed to the loss of life.

Whereas some persons perished quickly from disease and accidents, others lingered in sickness and pain before their deaths. In 1772 a twelve-year old orphan boy in Edgecombe County, Hardy Maund, remained ill for twelve days before succumbing. During that time expenses mounted for his two attendants, doctor, candles, and "the Trouble of the House"--the equivalent of bills for nurses, doctors, utilities, and hospital expenses.

Funerals were often gay, festive affairs no matter how decorous they were intended to be. Private burials were illegal in the colony; the law required at least three or four persons to witness the funeral of a deceased person. Thus the funeral was a public occasion which provided a reason, or an excuse, for the colonials to escape the solitude of their rural ways and enjoy companionship. The guests rarely exhibited the reverence ordinarily associated with funerals. The firing of guns, neighborly altercations, and general chatter made silence unusual.

Since many who attended funerals traveled great distances, food and drink had to be provided to satisfy their hunger and thirst. At the funeral of Mrs. Francis Corbin an observer reported that vast quantities of pork, beef, and cornbread, plus a hogshead of rum were set out for the guests. The quantity of rum at Hardy Maund's funeral was so inadequate that a man had to be sent to Tarboro twice for additional refreshments.

The extravagance of a funeral usually depended upon the wealth of the deceased individual or his family. Young Maund, for example, had received a large inheritance from his father which his guardian was quite willing to spend for funeral charges. However, there were those who were unwilling or unable to bear excessive charges. Dr. Cosmos Farguharson (Farquharson) of Wilmington instructed in his will that he should be buried without coffin, prayer, or ceremony and that his entire funeral should not cost more than forty shillings. Cornelius Harnett later agreed. That famous revolutionary noted that "as I have ever considered expensive funerals as ostentatious folly it is my earnest request (and from my present circumstances now doubly necessary) that I may be buried with the utmost frugality." Clearly the high cost of dying was a recognizable problem in the colonial era as it is today.

CHAPTER IV

RELIGION

The state of religion in colonial North Carolina remained unstable from the first settlements to the outbreak of the Revolution. The isolation of the colony, the change in ownership from the proprietors to the crown, and the continual immigration of disparate peoples contributed to the unsettled situation. Gov. William Tryon wrote in 1765 that every religious denomination except Catholicism abounded in the colony. However, the diversity of denominations did not ensure a religious populace. Anglican minister Charles Woodmason observed in the mid-1760s that "As to North Carolina, the State of Religion therein, is greatly to be lamented--If it can be said, That there is any Religion, or a Religious Person in it." As a partisan member of the Anglican church which was confronted with fierce sectarian competition, Woodmason, of course, exaggerated. Still, his assessment of the religious climate in North Carolina contained an element of truth.

Upon the founding of Carolina the lords proprietors had sanctioned religious toleration in order to entice immigrants to their colony, but at the same time they had given official encouragement to the Anglican church or Church of England. For thirty years the Anglicans remained unwilling or unable to take advantage of their privileged position. Not a single Anglican minister entered the province before 1700, and a well-organized Quaker faction dominated the religious scene.

By the turn of the eighteenth century the appointment of zealous Anglican governors and the appearance of Anglican missionaries from England upset the religious calm of the province. Legislation in 1701 and 1703 provided for the establishment of the Anglican church in the colony. Nevertheless, the superior status of the Church of England was not secured for another eight years. Quaker opposition to the establishment and the "rebellion" of former governor Thomas Cary in 1710-1711 delayed the implementation of the Anglican establishment. But in 1711 newly-appointed Gov. Edward Hyde, a distant cousin of Queen Anne, successfully repulsed Cary's armed resistance to the government and definitely confirmed the Anglican position.

The establishment apparently failed to redound to the benefit of the Anglicans. The church never evinced widespread strength or appeal in North Carolina. The proprietors continually slighted the province in favor of South Carolina, while after 1729, when the crown purchased North Carolina, the close association between the crown

St. Paul's Anglican Church in Edenton, one of the outstanding colonial churches, is still in use. Pictured above is Porte Crayon's sketch which appeared in *Harper's New Monthly Magazine*, 1866.

and the church often aroused hostile feelings. Non-Anglicans resented paying taxes for the support of the church, opposed the church's control over education, and decried other special privileges including the exclusive right of Anglican ministers to solemnize marriages. The ritual of the church, the failure to emphasize preaching, and aristocratic bias connoted a lack of emotional appeal which seriously curtailed the popularity of Anglicanism.

The absence of a resident bishop also retarded the growth of the Anglican church. North Carolina governors continually importuned London for a bishop to ordain prospective ministers, restrain clergymen who acted immoderately, and remove those guilty of malfeasance. The bishop of London and the crown spurned the requests, the consequence of which was twofold: a journey to England for ordination, a journey so long and dangerous that some prospective ministers perished; and a lack of restraint upon the clergy resident in America.

Of the less than fifty Anglican clergymen sent to North Carolina before 1775, the Society for the Propagation of the Gospel in Foreign Parts, founded in 1701 by the Reverend Thomas Bray and associates, dispatched thirty-three. The S.P.G. intended to send Anglican missionaries throughout the British empire for the purpose of offering divine worship and education to all English subjects including blacks and Indians; but the society slighted North Carolina, partly because the Carolinians seldom received missionaries very cordially and partly because physical dangers threatened those who challenged the Carolina wilderness. John Rainsford slept in an old tobacco barn, and

St. John's Church at Williamsborough, Vance County, was built during the years 1771-1773. Originally called Nutbush Church, St. John's was instigated by the vestry of St. Peter's nearby and built by John Lynch, according to the report submitted to the National Register of Historic Places. On this page are pictured various stages of restoration of the historic church, 1948-1956: top left, the church in 1947, showing alterations made at various times after its original construction; top right, restoration in progress--note the frame of the four original windows revealed after stripping away weatherboards; lower left, the building restored to its original simplicity; center right, exposed curved, barrel-type supports used in original construction of the nave; lower right, interior of the sanctuary after completion of restoration. Notable features include the box pews, raised pulpit, and chancel enclosed by communion rails. Photographs and information supplied by the Survey Unit, Division of Archives and History.

John Urmstone subsisted for some time on a dry crust of bread and salt water. The Reverend Ebenezer Taylor died as a result of remaining adrift in the Albemarle Sound for ten days in bitterly cold weather. The missionaries recognized the uninviting situation of the colony. In fact, John Blair called the province "the most barbarous place in the Continent" in 1704 and immediately departed from the area.

Despite the adverse geographic and climatic conditions, many able and conscientious ministers served the Anglican church in North Carolina. The Reverend Clement Hall, who officiated in St. Paul's Parish, Edenton, and the four northeastern counties in the colony from 1744 until his death in 1759, typified that group. In addition to preaching regularly in St. Paul's Parish, Hall usually journeyed through his mission territory at least twice a year. Seldom were his trips less than 200 miles, and on one occasion he traveled 557 miles in a 36-day period. In 1755 Hall estimated that he traveled 2,200 miles a year. He also went to Granville County and several times preached in Virginia in his efforts to reach those who desired the benefits of religious services. Hall's careful accounts of his labors indicated that he preached to congregations of as many as 600 persons, administered the Holy Communion to 300 persons on a single tour, and baptized at least 10,000 persons during his ministry.

While many of the clergymen were devoted, zealous, selfless individuals, there were others who were acknowledged scoundrels and whose activities besmirched the reputation of the entire ministry. Daniel Brett, the first Anglican minister in the colony, "brought great grief and shame to the friends of the Church" by his actions. The Reverend Michael Smith served the parishes in Johnston and New Hanover counties from 1758 to 1760 but was dismissed by the S.P.G. when his sordid past in South Carolina was revealed. In the southern colony he had lived with a woman without the benefit of marriage vows, retired to a tavern on Sundays after preaching, played billiards immediately after giving the Holy Sacrament, and defrauded his parish of considerable money. John Boyd of the Brunswick region in North Carolina was seen on a Sunday in the spring of 1737 "at noon day, . . . Lying dead Drunk & fast asleep on the Great Road to Virginia, with his Horse Bridle tyed to his Leg. . . ." About two years later it was reported that Boyd was dead and that he had died "in the same Beastly way he lived."

The quality of the Anglican ministry is understandable. North Carolina had little to offer the more able ministers. Salaries were always low and inflation continually reduced the value of such stipends. Although the vestries supposedly taxed the inhabitants to pay the ministers, often the vestries failed to levy the tax or the sheriffs who collected the moneys used the funds for their own purposes. The fact that most of the Anglican ministers were sent by the S.P.G. and partially maintained by the society indicated the lack of support rendered by the colonials. Furthermore, there were no outstanding parish churches to which ambitious young clergymen

could be appointed. In most of the parishes in the colony the majority of those claiming religious affiliation embraced some denomination
other than Anglicanism. Thus the Anglican ministers rarely received
the support of their parishes--moral or monetary. As the zealous
Anglican, Governor Tryon, lamented, there were no gradations of
church preferments, which was deplorable because "human industry is
generally excited by future prospects of reward in this world, as
well as by their hopes of greater in the next." Hence men of small
ablility, no influence, and often little religion accepted assign-
ments in North Carolina, and those reluctantly. As Thomas Parramore
has noted, "The appeal of North Carolina, by all accounts, might be
compared with that of Siberia for the subjects of the czar."

The growth and spread of dissenting sects--Quakers, Lutherans,
German Reformed, Dunkers (Church of the Brethren), Moravians, Pres-
byterians, Baptists, and Methodists--constituted a significant
development in North Carolina religious life during the royal era.
The Quakers represented the earliest element of organized religion
in the province. William Edmundson, a missionary, introduced Quakerism to the colony in 1672. When George Fox later arrived in the
Albemarle area, he found a small but thriving nucleus of Friends.
Since there was no other formal religion, church, or ministry in
North Carolina at the time, Fox had ample opportunity to make more
converts. Still, he and fellow missionaries had to endure severe
hardships. Roads were practically nonexistent, while fording the
many creeks and rivers was hazardous. Edmundson, on a second visit
to the province in 1676-1677, braved Indian hostilities along the
Virginia border in order to enter North Carolina.

The incidence of Quaker conversions increased rapidly and resulted in organized meetings at the regional and provincial levels.
The earliest monthly meeting was that held at the house of Francis
Toms in 1680. An Eastern Quarterly Meeting was established about
1681 for Friends in Pasquotank, Perquimans, and present-day Northampton counties. The first North Carolina Yearly Meeting was in-
stituted in 1698.

Although the number of Quakers in North Carolina is impossible
to determine exactly, several Anglican missionaries estimated their
adherents at one seventh to one tenth of the total population.
Those Anglicans characterized the Quakers as extremely ignorant,
insufferably proud, and ungovernable. However, it is possible to
discern a certain tacit admiration for the Quakers by the Anglican
ministers who appreciated their godliness and the ease with which
they made converts. And the Anglican clergy were forced to admit
that many embraced Quakerism in reaction to the poor example set by
the Anglicans, preferring any religion to none at all.

Between 1725 and 1775 a large migration of Quakers from Pennsylvania and more northerly areas contributed to an increase of
Friends in North Carolina as well as a broadening of the Quaker
geographical base in the colony. Early Quakerism was confined
principally to the Albemarle region though Quakers were scattered

throughout the eastern counties. The new immigrants settled in Alamance, Chatham, Guilford, Randolph, and Surry counties. One of the most influential of these settlements was New Garden in Guilford County which was established about 1750 and held a monthly meeting by that name in 1754. Most of the later Quaker meetings in the area emanated from the New Garden community. In 1771 an even larger migration of Quakers from Nantucket, Rhode Island, substantially increased the number of Friends in the middle portions of North Carolina. The influence of the Quakers continued to grow until the outbreak of the Revolution when hostilities curtailed the activities of the pacifistic Friends.

One of the early churches in the Piedmont was New Garden Meeting House in Guilford County, pictured from a sketch in Lossing, *The Pictorial Field Book of the Revolution*, II, 407.

Less important were the German sects which were prominent in the Piedmont. The Germans represented four sects primarily: Lutheran, Reformed, Dunkers, and Moravian. The Lutherans, probably the most numerous of the German sectaries, settled in Rowan, Cabarrus, Stanly, and Davidson among other central Piedmont counties. The Reformed adherents gravitated to the same communities. Both groups were without ministers upon their arrival in the colony in the late 1740s. The Reverend Christian Theus, a Reformed minister from South Carolina, preached in North Carolina in the 1750s and 1760s, and Samuel Suther later officiated at Grace Church in Rowan and the two other Reformed churches in Davidson. The Lutherans in the meantime had organized three churches--Zion and St. John's in Rowan and St. John's in Cabarrus County. In 1773 the Lutheran churches successfully secured a schoolmaster and minister from Germany, Johann Gottfried Arndt and Adolph Nussman respectively.

The Dunkers, whose name arose from the practice of total immersion, originated in Germany in 1708. Members of the sect attempted to imitate the Christians of the first century, which led them to adopt baptism by trine immersion, pacifism, rejection of courts to settle disputes, and great plainness in language and dress. The Dunkers established at least six settlements in North Carolina in the eighteenth century, but only two survived to become congregations in the twentieth century Church of the Brethren. The older is the Fraternity Church of the Brethren located six miles southwest of Winston-Salem; the other is the Flat Rock congregation of New River in Ashe County.

The Moravians were Protestants and followers of the Unitas Fratrum, mid-fifteenth century supporters of John Hus in Bohemia. The North Carolina Moravians were an offshoot of the Pennsylvania

Members of the Church of the Brethren were commonly called Dunkers. Pictured above is an old engraving which depicts German Dunkers on their way to the Shenandoah, reproduced from Julius Friedrich Sachse, *The German Sectarians of Pennsylvania: 1742-1800*, Volume II of *A Critical and Legendary History of the Ephrata Cloister and the Dunkers* (Philadelphia: Privately printed, 1900), II, 333. This photograph appeared in Roger E. Sappington, "Dunker Beginnings in North Carolina," *North Carolina Historical Review*, XLVI (Summer, 1969), 222.

group. Bishop Augustus Spangenberg led a party to survey prospective lands in North Carolina in 1752 for possible settlement. Subsequently 99,985 acres were purchased by the Moravians from Earl Granville in a tract which was called Wachovia. The first party of permanent Moravian settlers reached Wachovia in November, 1753. They and their successors inaugurated a thriving community which was designed to be a self-contained settlement wherein the Moravians could practice their social, religious, and economic customs.

The Scotch-Irish introduced Presbyterianism to North Carolina as an organized religion. William Robinson in 1742 was the first known Presbyterian minister to visit the colony, and he was followed by other itinerant preachers. The most famous of these missionaries was Hugh McAden, who left a detailed record of his endeavors. McAden first toured the colony in 1755 and 1756 at which time he encountered at least seven Presbyterian houses of worship and many worshiping communities but few organized churches and no resident ministers. McAden proceeded to visit some fifty communities where he usually preached in private homes or in open fields. He established at least seven churches between the Hyco and Yadkin rivers.

McAden persuaded the Reverend James Campbell to settle in the colony in 1758 to minister to the needs of the numerous Highland Scots living along the Cape Fear River. Campbell customarily preached two sermons on Sundays--one in Gaelic for the Highlanders and one in English for the less numerous Lowlanders and Scotch-Irish in the area. Campbell trained his listeners well for in 1770 the Reverend John McLeod said that he would rather preach to the most sophisticated congregation in Edinburgh than to "the little critical carls" along the Cape Fear.

Pictured here are, left to right, an early communion cup used by the Brethren deacons, a basin used for washing the hands after the foot-washing service and before the Love Feast, and a foot tub used for foot washing at the Love Feast and communion services. This photograph appeared in Roger E. Sappington, "Two Eighteenth Century Dunker Congregations," *North Carolina Historical Review*, XLVII (Spring, 1970), 185.

In 1758 the Reverend Alexander Craighead settled permanently in North Carolina. After Gen. Edward Braddock's disastrous defeat Indians had driven Craighead and his congregation from Virginia to North Carolina where they took refuge in Mecklenburg County. Craighead became pastor of the Rocky River and Sugar Creek churches and was the only Presbyterian minister between the Yadkin and Catawba rivers during the early 1760s.

McAden returned to the colony in 1759 to become the pastor of congregations in Duplin and New Hanover counties. Joining McAden, Campbell, and Craighead in the colony were such distinguished ministers as David Caldwell, Samuel E. McCorkle, and the particularly influential Henry Pattillo. In 1770 Presbyterians in North and South Carolina were organized into the Orange Presbytery which included twelve congregations in the two colonies. The Presbyterians in North Carolina organized at least forty-four churches in the province before 1780 and exercised an influence in the colony's politics, especially in the backcountry, far in excess of their proportionate numbers in the province.

Outstripping the Presbyterians and Quakers in popularity were the Baptists of one variety or another. While some individual Baptists may have been present in the colony in the seventeenth century, the first organized Baptist congregation appeared only in 1727, founded by the Reverend Paul Palmer near Cisco in Chowan County. The early congregations were General Baptists who offered salvation to all who repented and submitted to baptism. During the next two decades Baptist missionaries worked so effectively that by 1752 they claimed sixteen congregations and several hundred members. By the outbreak of the Revolution the Kehukee Baptist Association, formed in 1769 from churches in Halifax, Edgecombe, Martin, Washington, Beaufort, Carteret, other eastern counties, and a few South Carolina counties, alone accounted for sixty-one churches and 5,000 members.

In the 1750s the Separate Baptists challenged the older General Baptists. The Separates sprang from New England revivalism. The establishment of the Sandy Creek Church in 1755 in Guilford County by Shubal Stearns signaled the inauguration of the Separatist advent in North Carolina. These Baptists stressed the autonomy of each congregation and weekly communion, believed in nine Christian rites including the Lord's Supper and Baptism, and accepted "eldresses" and "deaconesses." Their religious gatherings, often in the camp meeting style, frequently culminated in fits, frenzied jerkings, talking in tongues, and other expressions of zeal which alarmed persons of the more conservative denominational persuasions. Whereas the General Baptists had sought converts, they had not offended the Anglicans in the process. The Separates were not so reserved, and their appeal seemed irresistible. In 1758 the Sandy Creek Association, the oldest Baptist association in North Carolina, was formed and within two decades there were at least forty-two Separate churches in the colony. By 1775 the Baptists probably constituted the most numerous group of religious adherents in North Carolina and presented the most formidable opposition to the established Anglican church.

The last major Protestant denomination to secure a foothold in North Carolina before the Revolution was Methodism. A product of John Wesley's religious experience and maturation, Methodism had been an organized movement in England thirty years before its missionaries were sent to America. Between 1769 and 1774 Wesley dispatched to the colonies eight such emissaries, of whom Francis Asbury remained to become the father of American Methodism.

Methodism was immediately popular in the Middle Atlantic and southern colonies, particularly in Virginia and North Carolina. Relatively democratic church organization, a degree of local autonomy, and evangelical fervor enhanced its appeal. The failure of the established church to minister to the spiritual needs of the people and the existence of a large number of churchless inhabitants contributed to the success of the Methodist movement.

The first Methodist minister to reach North Carolina was Joseph Pilmore who preached a sermon in the province on September 12, 1772, at the Currituck County courthouse. Two years later North Carolina Methodists were sufficiently numerous to be included in the first Virginia circuit, which extended from Petersburg to the Albemarle counties. By 1776 North Carolina's 683 Methodists justified a circuit of their own. By that time northeastern North Carolina and southern Virginia had become the cradle of southern Methodism in one of the biggest revivals ever experienced by the Methodist church in America.

Despite the establishment of the Anglican church and the rapid strides made by the dissenting sects, North Carolinians remained a comparatively unchurched people, as the Methodists had found in the 1770s. Contemporary Virginia historian Hugh Jones in *The Present State of Virginia* wrote that "Religion cannot be expected among a Collection of such People as fly thither from other Places for Safety and Livelihood, left to their own Liberty without Restraint or Instruction." Many had "but the bare name of God and Christ; and that too frequently in nothing but vain Swearing, Cursing, and Imprecations."

The exception to such unseemly behavior was the Moravian settlement at Wachovia. This group through organized and cooperative effort succeeded in establishing a Christian community, aiding their neighbors, and spreading the gospel on the very edge of the frontier. The deep sense of religion within the Moravian settlement spoke for itself, but equally laudable was their attempt to minister to the needs of other Christians in the area who were without benefit of church or clergy. When English-speaking visitors were present in Wachovia, services would be held in English. Moravians also visited neighbors in their homes and held services for them. They freely administered baptismal rites to children but never claimed by such action that the children were members of the Moravian church. Had the Moravians attempted to convert other North Carolinians, they might have been quite successful. But they were satisfied to bring the gospel to those in need and allow others to reap the fertile religious harvest which they sowed.

The North Carolina government attempted to remedy the lax moral situation by statute, but the difficulties of legislating morality were quickly perceived. At least as early as 1715 the provincial assembly enacted legislation to encourage the observance of Sunday as a holy day. The law directed everyone to engage in some form of private or public worship on Sunday and forbade any labor including hunting and fishing on the Sabbath. Slaves were similarly restricted in their activities.

The legislators also noted that "the odious & loathsome Sin of Drunkenness" had become a common occurrence in the colony. Since this was the foundation of many iniquitous practices, the law contained a provision for levying fines on those who became intoxicated on the Sabbath. Furthermore, tavern keepers were forbidden to sell any alcoholic beverages on Sundays except to travelers. Later this restriction was relaxed to permit the sale of liquors on Sundays before and after church hours but tavern keepers were warned not to allow anyone to become drunk.

The legislation of 1715 contained further admonitions against other prevalent immoral activities. Profane cursing, mentioned by Jones, and common-law marriages were prohibited. A similar statute in 1741 reiterated many of the provisions of the earlier law and pointedly observed that clergymen in the colony were not exempt from the penalties of the law.

Despite the laws many North Carolinians remained ignorant of religion. This seemed particularly true in the backcountry where the inhabitants were somewhat isolated and civilization was in its elementary stages. The people of western North Carolina were occupied by the rigors of building homes and extracting livelihoods from the wilderness. They often lived and behaved in the manner of the Indians with whom they vied for the land. Thus a polished, learned, and godly individual such as the Reverend Woodmason might easily declare that the manners of North Carolinians were vile and corrupt, that the colony was a scene of debauchery and dissoluteness, and that the people lived in a state of polygamy, illegitimacy, and concubinage.

The situation in the east was only slightly better than in the backcountry. Josiah Quincy, Jr., the intercolonial traveler and journalist from Massachusetts, noted that many of the political and social leaders of the Cape Fear area ignored the laws relative to religion and the observance of the Sabbath. He concluded that it was time either to repeal such laws or to attempt a better execution of them. That his observations had some merit was supported by the necessity of having the constables of Beaufort and Wilmington patrol the streets on Sundays near the places of worship during church hours to disperse persons who were noisy and disturbed the worshipers. However, in Wilmington the constables were remiss in their duty, an indication of their less than faithful observance of the Sabbath Day.

A folding money scale such as this one (circa 1790) was useful to colonials in detecting counterfeit coin. The pocket coin balances served to test the authenticity of gold and silver coin. The scale was usually quite small and could be folded neatly into a pocket-size case. Opened, the scale looked like the one carried by the classical figure depicted on the inside of the case. Note the pyramid of weights pictured. Photograph copied from Geoffrey Wills, *Copper and Brass* (London: Billing & Sons, Ltd., 1968), 90, and used in the *North Carolina Historical Review* (Summer, 1973), 241.

This state of religion was hardly surprising. Religion throughout the southern colonies as well as in England appeared to have been lackluster in its appeal and influence in the mid-eighteenth century. In North Carolina the populace was very poor and unable to support adequately church construction and ministers of any denomination. Even such outstanding preachers as Henry Pattillo died penniless, though in his case congregations were not entirely to blame, while churches rotted, stood half-finished, or became shelters for hogs and cattle. Difficulties of travel and communication, particularly severe in North Carolina, hampered all social interaction including religious gatherings. This condition was reinforced by the lack of large urban centers in the colony which congregated people and fostered cultural development as in New England.

Nevertheless, the more positive aspects of religious development in the colony should not be overlooked. The vestries within the Anglican parishes performed valuable social as well as religious functions. For a time they kept the standards of weights and measures for their respective counties: in 1703 the vestry in St. Paul's Parish in Chowan purchased a brass yard, a pair of brass scales, a one-gallon pewter wine pot, a half bushel, a peck, and a quart pot. Vestries also cared for the sick, aged, and orphaned within their bounds. Such persons were lodged with families able to care for them in the parishes.

Some churches made attempts to carry the elements of Christianity to the blacks and Indians in the colony. The first S.P.G. missionaries sincerely tried to convert the blacks, but they were partially thwarted by the prevailing contention among planters that the baptism of a slave constituted his liberation. This belief slowly eroded during the proprietary era and by the 1730s Anglican ministers began to baptize slaves; yet the conversion to Christianity did not change the status of the slaves and failed to alter materially the masters' attitudes toward their bondsmen.

Before 1741 blacks were allowed to join a church but were forbidden to organize a church for members of their race. A solely black church represented a center for the practice of other than Christian rites or for possible conspiracies on the part of the slaves. A statute in 1741 regulating the practice of slavery, however, omitted that provision though it is unlikely that a widespread black church organization arose.

Denominations other than Anglican also took cognizance of the potential reservoir of Christians represented by the blacks. The Baptists apparently received blacks into their congregations, but the Quakers were the first sect to try to put their religious principles into practice and alter the slaves' status. Quakers owned slaves during the colonial period but became increasingly uneasy about the practice. At their monthly, quarterly, and annual meetings they began to question the treatment received by slaves of Friends, the necessity of buying and selling slaves by Friends, and in 1769 the desirability of owning slaves. In 1776, when white Americans launched their attempt to free themselves from their yoke of slavery to King George III, Quakers in North Carolina upheld the spirit of emancipation by announcing their intention to free their black slaves.

Attempts to convert the Indians were less successful. Early Anglican missionaries spoke of meetings with the Indians and their chiefs. Some seemed amenable to conversion to Christianity but there is little indication of the widespread acceptance of Christianity by the Indians. Most of the interest in the Indians consisted of the efforts to combat the influence of the French and Catholicism along the frontier. Perhaps the most notable contribution on the part of the whites was made by the Reverend Alexander Stewart who preached to the remnants of the Mattamuskeet, Roanoke, and Hatteras Indians in the Hyde County area. He baptized twenty-one of the Indians on one occasion and established a school for the Indians and the blacks in the area.

Although the missionary impulse was a stimulus to the colonization of English America, whites experienced difficulty in their desire to Christianize the Indians. Unlike the blacks, the Indians presented an element of militant opposition, more particularly when they colluded with the French. The settlers found it easier to call the Indians a heathen people and wage war against them. The exceptions to this observation were those Indians to whom the Reverend Stewart ministered who were effectively settled on reservations and presented no threat to the whites.

In addition to the attempts of clergymen to minister to the needs of the people, the efforts of individual lay Christians should not be overlooked. Sincere Christians undertook to support their churches and parishes by their time, effort, and money. At his death Henderson Walker left money for the construction of a church and ten barrels of corn to be distributed equally among ten poor people in his area. Wilmington merchant John Paine ordered his executors to pay Ŀ13 to the churchwardens in each county in the province for the benefit of the poor. Others left money for the construction of churches both in North Carolina and in their native European countries such as Ireland and Scotland. The most munificent gift was Alexander Duncan's bequest of Ŀ400 for the finishing or adornment of St. James Church in Wilmington. Clearly, religion was not defunct in the colony. North Carolinians had made remarkable progress in the realization of the benefits of organized religion in the century preceding the Revolution.

CHAPTER V

TRANSPORTATION AND COMMUNICATION

Transportation in colonial North Carolina was often slow, difficult, and hazardous. The early settlers found that the numerous swamps and general sparseness of population hindered the construction and maintenance of suitable highways in the province. Thus, in the seventeenth and early eighteenth centuries the colonials depended greatly upon water transport provided by the streams, creeks, and rivers in the coastal area. Settlers purchased land on these watercourses for purposes of personal travel and the transportation of agricultural produce. Private and public landings dotted the major creeks and rivers in the Albemarle section.

Carolinians used various types of boats to ply their inland waterways. Canoes were a popular and versatile craft. Generally made of cypress, the canoes varied in size from those which carried only one or two passengers to those which transported two or three horses. Smaller canoes were propelled by paddles or oars, while larger ones might be equipped with sails. John Brickell found that "no Boat in the World is capable to be rowed as fast as they are, and when they are full of Water they will not sink. . . ."

Settlers emigrating from Virginia into Albemarle County frequently followed streams and rivers which abounded in the eastern area. From Hugh T. Lefler and William S. Powell, *Colonial North Carolina: A History* (New York: Charles Scribner's Sons, 1973), 45. Reproduced by courtesy of the authors and the North Carolina Collection, University of North Carolina.

Piraguas, larger than canoes, were made from hollowed cypress logs which were widened by splitting the logs to add one or more planks. Oars and sails propelled these boats, which could transport as many as 100 barrels of pitch and tar or several horses. Early in the colonial era the provincials used piraguas in the coastal trade but after 1750 larger, more seaworthy vessels replaced them. Brickell observed that no European boat of the same size could out-sail a Carolina piragua.

Scows and flats exceeded piraguas in size. These were flat-bottomed boats designed principally for inland commerce. They were shallow-draft vessels which could carry large quantities of lumber, shingles, corn, tobacco, pitch, and tar. Carolinians also used various other boats for water transportation. Small sloops or shallops were employed on the sounds and large rivers though such craft were reported as far inland as Halifax on the Roanoke River in 1774. Yawls and bayboats occasionally appeared on the inland waters along with pleasure craft as the boat, complete with awnings and six uniformed slaves, which conveyed Janet Schaw down the North-east Cape Fear to Wilmington.

As the sites along the waterways were preempted and the inhab-itants of the province moved inland, more and better roads became mandatory. At first, many of the routes were constructed simply to connect interior plantations to public landings, but eventually roads were necessary for various aspects of intracounty transportation. Intracounty roads soon gave way to intercounty highways as a colo-nial road network emerged. By 1775 maps of North Carolina indicated an intricate transportation system wherein the longer routes were connected by innumerable shorter roads.

Authorization for the construction of roads emanated from the provincial assembly and the various county courts. The few roads projected by the legislature were designed to facilitate intercounty travel, particularly for purposes of promoting trade. The county courts supervised the building of the vast majority of provincial highways. Generally, the justices entertained petitions by those living in the counties for roads to public landings, churches, schools, courthouses, and mills. If the courts approved such peti-tions, as they usually did, they appointed twelve men to mark the proposed route and designated certain residents of the area to clear and maintain the road. All able-bodied males, white and black, were responsible for the construction and repair of the roads.

The most important provincial roads included the King's High-way which passed through Edenton, Bath, New Bern, and Wilmington and the inland variation of that route which came from Virginia through Halifax and Tarboro to New Bern. In the west major trading routes ran from the Wachovia tract to Petersburg, Virginia, and to Charles-ton, South Carolina. The principal east-west roads passed from New Bern, Wilmington, and Cross Creek to the western counties of Guil-ford, Rowan, and Mecklenburg. Countless shorter roads connected the major highways and intercounty routes.

From Tatham, Tobacco (1800)

Primitive but effective modes of transporting tobacco and other produce out of the colony are illustrated above: (a) Two parallel piraguas or canoes could be used as a raft by placing boards across and using the two vessels as one; (b) a single upland boat was sometimes feasible; (c) a wagon was practical for long journeys; (d) a hogshead with two hoops added could be rolled to market. Photograph of a sketch by W. Newman, from William Tatum, *An Historical and Practical Essay on the Culture and Commerce of Tobacco* (London: Printed for Vernon and Hood, 31, Poultry, by T. Bensley, Bolt Court, Fleet Street, 1800); reprinted in facsimile in G. Melvin Herndon, *William Tatum and the Culture of Tobacco* (Coral Gables, Florida: University of Miami Press, 1969), facing 55.

Special types of road construction were used for some of the shorter roads. Bridle roads, bridle paths, or "by-ways," narrower than the regularly authorized roads, were commonly used to reduce the expense and time of clearing a road of normal width. These roads were designed to connect a person's house or mill with a main road, a landing with a main road, or as a means of joining two highways. Causeways or "causeys" were means of crossing lowlands, swamps, or pocosins. Frequently they were also constructed at ferry landings. The colonials built causeways by placing logs in the direction of the road, covering them with dirt, and covering this with small pine trees, brush, and dirt again. Usually the causeways were higher in the center and tapered to the edges to ensure a proper drainage of water.

North Carolina roads were exceptionally narrow by European standards and rarely failed to register a negative impression on foreign travelers. The principal exception was the highway north of Wilmington leading to the Northeast Cape Fear River, which was wide enough for fifty men to march abreast. The roads in the colony were also cut in all different points of the compass and were often little more than blazed paths through the woods. The blazes or notches on the sides of trees became difficult to discern after a number of years. Compounding a traveler's difficulty was the fact that many roads were little distinguished from animal paths and Indian paths. Guides were often necessary, though early in the colonial era it was not uncommon for guides to lose their way.

In 1764 the assembly ordered that the major roads in the province be posted and measured. The appearance of Five Mile posts and Three Fingers posts along the roads attested to at least partial compliance with the law. When riding from Bath to New Bern one traveler commented on the signposts with the number of miles marked in Roman numerals and notches, the latter, he supposed, for the benefit of the unlearned. Despite the assistance of signposts and markers, many lost their way. One man spent the night in the woods between Brunswick and Wilmington combatting wolves. Another took a short cut in the same area, and after losing his way, noted in a very positive manner in his journal never to take any more short cuts in North Carolina.

Although the fortunate traveler might stay on the road, a satisfactory trip was not thereby ensured. In the eastern counties the reads often consisted of deep, loose, white sand which slowed travel and tired horses. Occasionally the sand concealed tree roots which tripped horses. The traveler also feared the many dead trees which lined the roadsides and could fall with thundering crashes during strong winds. This threat was the result of the colonial practice of boxing pines to obtain turpentine or burning forests to clear land.

Travel through North Carolina proved lonely, dull, and annoying at times. One could ride an entire day without meeting anyone or seeing a house. A traveler once commented that "Nothing can be more dreary, melancholy and uncomfortable than the almost perpetual solitary dreary pines, sandy barrens, and dismal swamps" throughout eastern North Carolina. That tiresome, unvaried scene was compounded by frightening encounters with numerous snakes and pesky mosquitoes.

The principal mode of transportation was the horse. It was said that the colonial would gladly walk five miles to catch his horse even for a ride of only one mile. The necessity for walking such a distance, if that was the case, stemmed from the fact that Carolinians often bestowed little care on their horses. They allowed the animals to roam loose in the woods and forage for themselves. Bishop Augustus Spangenburg observed that at the end of the winter the horses were so emaciated they were of little benefit to their owners during the spring and summer months.

Travel by horse was certainly the most rapid means of transportation. An average of thirty miles per day was considered a satisfactory journey. However, a rider might attempt fifty miles in a day though he and his horse would be greatly fatigued by such a trip. In 1779 Whitmill Hill, a delegate to the Continental Congress from North Carolina, traversed the distance from Philadelphia to his home in Martin County in the remarkable time of seven and one-half days.

For transporting all but the lightest commodities a wagon or cart was necessary. Wagons were less numerous than carts and seemed to have been used mostly in the backcountry. Two or four horses pulled the wagons, which could carry an average load of 2,000 pounds. Wagons proved indispensable for trading and mercantile operations in the Piedmont area. The Moravians carried on an extensive trade with Charleston, Brunswick, New Bern, and Petersburg with such vehicles. Wagons also brought countless immigrants from the northern colonies and South Carolina into western North Carolina.

The cart was the predominant work vehicle throughout the colony. On the short-bodied, two-wheeled cart the planter could haul his produce to market, grain and fodder around the farm, and his family to church. So valuable was the cart that even the wheels were saved when the body was discarded. Such vehicles could carry average loads of 1,000 pounds.

Less common were several types of wheeled vehicles whose cost restricted their ownership to the wealthy in the colony. The sulky and gig were light, one-passenger carriages; the chair and chaise, light, two-passenger, and two- or four-wheeled carriages; the post-chaise, a four-wheeled chaise; the chariot, similar to the post-chaise but having a coach box; the phaeton, a light, open, four-wheeled carriage; and the coach, a large, closed, four-wheeled carriage. The sulky and chair were the most prevalent wheeled carriages and could travel almost as fast as a horseman on the better roads of the province. Generally the poor condition of most of the roads discouraged the use of such vehicles until approximately two decades before the Revolution. Actually, few Carolinians traveled great distances anyway. Most limited their trips to visiting neighbors, going to church, hauling produce or driving livestock to market, and going to the courthouse on public occasions. Only the wealthier planters, merchants, lawyers, judges, assemblymen, clergymen, and itinerant peddlers spent much time in extensive travel.

The numerous streams, creeks, and rivers in the colony necessitated crossings by means of fords, bridges, and ferries. Narrower and shallower waters in the backcountry made fording easier in the Piedmont region than along the coast where "impenetrable swamps and bottomless morasses" hindered such activities. Fords were natural crossings for roads and a few fords were eventually bridged to eliminate the inconvenience of wading or swimming through waters with animals, carts, and wagons. Bridges were also constructed at private docks or landings, mills, and former ferry sites.

Provincial legislation provided general instructions for the building of bridges and the county courts added the details. A typical bridge was at least twelve feet wide. It consisted of fifteen-inch pilings driven into the stream bed. Sills or sleepers were set into them and braced with timbers seven by five inches thick. The floor was made of sawed boards "clear of sap" and at least two inches thick. It was about five to seven feet above the water. The bridge had one or two protective rails on each side which were three by four inches thick. Cypress was used extensively for bridge construction in the eastern counties. If a bridge survived the frequent floods, or freshets as they were called, its average lifetime was ten to fifteen years.

The men who constructed and repaired the roads also built the bridges. In 1745, however, the legislature permitted some counties to contract with private individuals to build bridges at the expense of the county taxpayers. Later this privilege was extended to all the counties in the province. Often the county courts required the contractors to keep bridges repaired for as many as seven years after the completion of the structures. The cost of erecting such bridges ranged from only ₺4 for one over a small stream in Bute County to the large sum of ₺190 for the bridge over the Tar River at Tarboro in Edgecombe County, which was one of the most impressive bridges in the colony.

Private toll bridges supplemented the public facilities. On rare occasions the assembly authorized individuals to construct bridges and charge travelers stipulated rates for the use of the bridges. Cumberland County also followed that practice. The county court permitted the private bridgekeepers to charge the usual ferry rates on the rivers over which the bridges were built but demanded that persons on public business be allowed to pass free of charge.

North Carolina possessed at least two drawbridges, a type of bridge construction which was rare in colonial America. The oldest and best known was that of Capt. Benjamin Heron, who was authorized by the assembly to build a drawbridge over the Northeast Cape Fear just north of present Castle Hayne. Heron's bridge opened in the middle by a system of pulleys. The other drawbridge was constructed over

the Cashie River at Windsor in Bertie County by order of the Bertie
County court. Prominent residents of New Bern and Craven County attempted to raise enough money by private subscriptions to build a
drawbridge over the Trent River at Swimming Point but the Revolution
interrupted their efforts.

When fording and bridging proved inadequate means to cross
watercourses, the colonials resorted to ferries. A scattered population and restricted mobility resulting from poor roads retarded

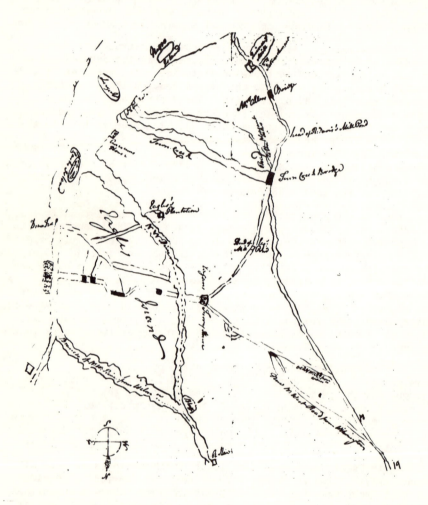

A pen-and-ink sketch indicates the roads and ferries in Brunswick and New
Hanover counties. Points noted are Eagles Island, Wilmington, and the areas
inland from the Cape Fear River to about four miles west. Photograph made
from copy in the Map Collection, State Archives, Raleigh. The original manuscript is in the William L. Clements Library at the University of Michigan.

the development of the ferriage service in North Carolina. As late as 1745 there appeared to be no regular ferriage transportation from Edenton across the Albemarle Sound. However, by the 1760s ferry service had been established throughout the eastern counties.

The more westerly counties had less need of ferriage since their waters could often be forded or bridged. Still, the Northeast Cape Fear, Tar, Haw, Catawba, and Yadkin rivers occasioned ferry crossings, and the establishment of ferries was of prime concern to the inhabitants in the vicinity of those rivers. By the end of the colonial period North Carolina probably possessed a sufficient number of ferries for its transportation network though the quality of ferriage service may have been questionable.

The creation of ferries proceeded principally from two sources of authority--the provincial assembly and the county courts. The county courts issued most of the ferry licenses. When authorizing ferry service, the courts determined the location of the ferry, boats required for transport, rates charged for passage, and bonds for ensuring proper performance of duties by ferrykeepers. Boats used for ferriage included canoes, piraguas, flats, and scows. Along the coast these vessels were usually in poor condition. The one at the Neuse River at New Bern was once described as "very bad." At Snead's Ferry over New River the boat was an "ordinary bauble" which floated no more than two or three inches above the water. William Dry's boats on either side of Eagles Island in the Cape Fear opposite Wilmington were leaky craft in which passengers were often soaked in their crossings of the river. In the interior counties, however, the quality of ferry boats improved greatly.

In addition to boats some ferrykeepers kept pastures for the grazing of horses while the animals and their owners awaited passage. The New Hanover County Court in 1760 ordered all ferrymen in the county to furnish pens or pounds for detaining cattle and forcing them into the water. Late in the colonial period thought was given to the owners of these animals. The assembly required ferrykeepers at the longer ferriage points to maintain taverns so that travelers might refresh themselves as they waited.

Delays at ferries were commonplace. If the ferry boat was on the opposite side of the water, the prospective passenger gave notice of his presence by ringing a bell provided for that purpose or by yelling across the water. Yet, service was not always forthcoming. Ebenezer Hazard once found that the ferryman at Bath had "run away." And the weather compounded the errors of man. Adverse winds and waters might delay passage at the wider ferries--such as the Albemarle Sound crossing--for two or three days. The Reverend Joseph Pilmore recorded his detention on Eagles Island during a thunderstorm in March, 1773, which greatly frightened him. He feared that he might have to spend the night on the island, but the storm abated late in the afternoon to permit him to shout for the boat in Wilmington.

The legislature gave impetus to public transportation in North Carolina in 1741 by instituting a system of free ferriage for persons traveling across New River from White House Point to Johnston, the newly created town and county seat of Onslow County. The free ferry proved so advantageous that the court continued its operation after the location of the county seat was moved to Wantland's Ferry (now Jacksonville). The assembly followed the Johnston experiment with legislation in 1754 and 1758 establishing free ferries across the Perquimans and Pasquotank rivers to facilitate travel to and from the courthouses of the counties during court sessions, election of members of the vestry and assembly, and the gathering of musters. Eventually the counties of Hertford, Rowan, Mecklenburg, Pitt, Tyrrell, and Anson were permitted to establish free ferry transportation. At least two counties, Cumberland and Bertie, also supervised the operation of ferries at public expense but without legislative authorization.

The ferries often assumed a role of importance in the communications of the colony. Coupled with the poor quality of many of the roads, the longer ferries at Edenton, Bath, New Bern, and Wilmington proved a hindrance to the establishment of regular postal service in North Carolina. Ferries also detained members of the assembly, which obstructed legislative business and possibly determined the contest for speaker of the house in 1754. Chief Justice Martin Howard noted that the "many wide and dangerous ferrys" hampered the administration of justice and helped make his office more burdensome and expensive than any on the continent. The ferries also hindered the ministerial activities of the many itinerant preachers in the colony. Clearly provincial ferries exerted considerable influence, often adverse, upon many facets of colonial life.

Communication in colonial North Carolina rested heavily upon oral transmission. Illiteracy, difficulties of transportation, and inadequate postal facilities prevented widespread reliance upon the written word. The tradition of southern hospitality stemmed in part from the desire for good conversation and news from the outside world. Travelers of the upper class were eagerly sought by their counterparts in North Carolina. Hosts pleaded with their guests to remain for weeks while they plied their visitors for the latest international and intercolonial developments.

The lower classes were not unfriendly. In fact, a marked characteristic of all such American colonials was their inordinate curiosity. To the upper-or middle-class travelers such inquisitiveness bordered on impertinence but actually it was the result of a desire for information about the external world. Many colonials traveled no more than fifty miles from their place of birth during their lifetimes. Some were so ignorant that they could not have named the reigning monarchs of England.

Written communications consisted principally of letters and newspapers. Lacking other means of communication colonials became adept and comprehensive letter writers. The techniques of writing

November 15, 1751.　THE　[Number 4.]

North CAROLINA GAZETTE.

I.e. the freshest Advices, Foreign and Domestic.

All Persons may be supplied with this PAPER, at *Four Shillings*, Proclamation Money, *per* Quarter, by JAMES DAVIS, at the Printing-Office in *Newbern*; where all Manner of Printing-Work, and Book-Binding, is done reasonably. ADVERTISEMENTS of a moderate Length, are inserted for *Three Shillings* the first Week, and *Two Shillings* for every Week after.

The TEMPLE of HYMEN. A VISION.

A Few Days ago I had an Account of the Marriage of a Friend. When Occurrences of this Nature make an Impression upon the Mind, it is insensibly betrayed into little Animadversions upon them. This was my Case in an extraordinary Manner; for having raised some time on this Incident, I fell into an easy Slumber, when Fancy resumed the Subject, and sallied out in the following Vision.

I thought I was in an Instant placed on the Boundaries of a spacious Plain; in the Center of which was presented to the Eye a large Temple consecrated to *Hymen*, the God of Marriage. At a small Distance from me I observed a giddy Crowd of both Sexes, who were making towards the Building, in order to celebrate the Ceremony of the God. There was stationed amongst them, a Dæmon, whose Form was so peculiar, and whose Sway with the Multitude so universal, that I shall here give my Reader a particular Description of him. It seems the Name of this Fury was *Lust*; in his upper Part of his Body, he carried the Likeness of a human Figure; from the Middle downwards he wore the Resemblance of a Goat, his Eyes were turgid, sparkling, and inflamed, his Complexion was very irregular, attended with the most sudden Transitions from a sanguine Red to a livid Paleness, and a Tremor frequently seiz'd every Member. Close followed him *Disease*, with a sickly Countenance and superstitious Eye; and *Remorse*, with his Hat flapped over his Face, and a Worm gnawing his Vitals. I was shocked at these monstrous Appearances, and the more so, to observe how readily my Fellow-Creatures gave into the impious Suggestions of the Dæmon. But my Surprize was somewhat abated on a nearer Approach; for I took notice that his Breath was of such a malignant Nature, that all those who rashly advanced within its Influence, were presently intoxicated, and deprived of their Reason.

I was in such a Consternation at this Discovery, that I hesitated for a while, whether I should enter into Conversation with the little Adventurers formerly mentioned. In the midst of my Suspence there came towards us a grave old Gentleman of a steady and composed Aspect, whose Name was *Deliberation*. He was one of the principal Agents belonging to the Temple, and so high in the God's Esteem, that *Hymen* was very rarely known to give his Benediction at a Confirmation of the Ceremony to any Couple who were not others, into his Presence, by this venerable Officer. Upon his joining the Company (to the Mistery Of which I found he was a perfect Stranger) there was expressed an universal Uneasiness and Discontent; and many of them, industriously avoided all Conversation with him. But it was very remarkable that all those, who thus imprudently turned their Backs on this valuable Minister, in their Return from the Temple, were seized by one or both of the melancholy Attendants of the Fury.

At my Entrance into the Building, I observed the Deity marching at a small Distance towards it.—The first in the Procession was *Love*, in the Form of a *Cupid*, who was continually practising a thousand little Arts and Graces, to draw upon him the Smiles of the God; and by the tender Regards which *Hymen* cast upon the Child, I found he was a very great Favourite. The God followed next, holding in his Hand a flaming

Torch; which shone the brighter the longer it burn'd; he approach'd to supper, by *Virtue*, a Lady of the most engaging Form that I had ever beheld. She was clouthed in a white refulgent Garment, and her Head was encircled with Glory.

The next Attendant was *Beauty*, arrayed in the most gorgeous Apparel, and full of herself, even to Distraction. She was handed along by *Youth*, a gay Stripling, wearing a Chaplet of Flowers on his Head, and Wings on his Shoulders.

Then appeared *Wealth* in the Figure of an old Man, meanly attired; his Eyes were the Eyes of a Hawk, and his Fingers curved and pointed inwards, like the Talons of a Raven; He was noisy, impudent, and presuming. The Retinue was closed by *Fancy*, ever varying her Features and Dress; and what was very extraordinary, methought the charm'd in all.

The Deity immediately after his Entrance into the Temple, ascended his Throne; and sat with his Head gently reclin'd on *Virtue*'s Bosom. *Love*, and *Beauty*, took their Station on the Right Hand; and on the Left, were disposed *Wealth* and *Fancy*.

The God quickly proceeded to the Celebration of the Nuptial Rites; but there was such a confused Sound of Sighs and Laughter, that I could not give the Attention which was requisite, in order to present my Reader with the several Circumstances that occurred; only I took Notice, that many of the Matches were so very unequal, that the God yoked them with Reluctance, and but half consented to his own Institution.

After the Ceremony was over, Silence was proclaimed in Court; for *Hymen* was determined to decide a Contest, which had been of long standing, between the Personages that attended the Altar. Upon this Declaration, the whole Multitude divided, and according to the particular Impulses of their Passions, took the Party of the several Competitors. The Young had ranked themselves on the right Hand of the Throne, while others of more advanced Years, had posted themselves behind the Disputants on the Left.

Love began with entering his Complaint against *Wealth*; setting forth, that his Antagonist had seduced such large Numbers to his Sentiments; that as to himself, his Interest very visibly declined every Day; to the great Prejudice of that State, wherein the Gods had design'd him the Pre-heminence.—While he was pushing his Arguments with great Warmth, *Poverty* stepp'd forth from amidst the Croud, and stared the young Plaintiff full in the Face; who was so frighten'd at his sorrowful Countenance, that he fluttered his Pinions in order for Flight. When *Wealth* rising up addressed the Judges, with shewing the Necessity of his Presence, to make the Married State so replete with Happiness, as it was originally intended by its Institute; together with many other Arguments, which, if they had been delivered with the same Modesty and Force, could not have failed of creating a Multitude of Converts to his Side. This his Speech was followed with a under—of Applause from the Company behind. Upon this Incident the old Man began to triumph, and to resume his Discourse; when, through the Violence of his Emotions, his Garment flew open, and betrayed to View, *Cares* in the Form of Vultures, hanging at his Breast. Hereupon *Love* stood up, and would fain have resumed his Cause. But *Hymen*, who well knew that the Presence of both was of the utmost Importance in the Performance of his Institution; and

For four shillings a quarter in 1751 anyone could subscribe to the *North Carolina Gazette*. Featured in the November 15 edition was an essay, "The Temple of Hymen. A Vision." From the files of the Division of Archives and History.

71

and the art of calligraphy were more highly developed than in the twentieth century, and the correspondent included far more general news than modern composers of letters. When Peter DuBois of Wilmington wrote to his friend Samuel Johnston of Edenton in 1757, he observed that two English squadrons were outfitting for a secret mission, that the Russians had been denied a passage through Poland, that the king of Prussia remained firm in his alliance, that the Byng trial had begun in England, and that Parliament intended to impeach several highly-placed officials.

Newspapers were an important channel of communication in the colonial era, but North Carolina was one of the last colonies to benefit from this medium of information. The first paper, the *North Carolina Gazette*, was published in New Bern in 1751. Thereafter the *North Carolina Magazine; or, Universal Intelligencer* (New Bern), the *North Carolina Gazette* (Wilmington), and the *Cape Fear Mercury* (Wilmington) served the colony before the Revolution. These papers carried mostly international news and but little intercolonial and local material. Of course the releases were dated because three to ten months elapsed between the occurrence of events in the northern colonies or England and the reports in the North Carolina newspapers. Nevertheless, the papers were eagerly awaited by the provincials, who scrutinized their contents and read them to the less literate. Thus, newspapers probably reached an audience which was four to five times the number of subscribers.

The lack of an adequate postal system in the colony before the Revolution was a major factor explaining the slowness and difficulty of communications. Only in 1770 was a regular postal service realized. Before 1770 Carolinians relied upon friends, expresses, or private carriers, and packet boats in the coastal trade to transport letters and papers. Expresses were expensive and their cost deterred sending all but important correspondence by that means. Friends or private individuals and packets, however, were generally slower and less reliable than expresses.

Gov. William Tryon was responsible for the creation of a systematic postal service for the colony. When he succeeded Governor Dobbs in 1765, North Carolina was the only English province along the seaboard which lacked postal facilities. A gap existed in postal communications from Suffolk, Virginia, to Charleston, South Carolina. Vigorous prodding of the North Carolina assembly and frequent correspondence with the governors of Virginia and South Carolina and British postal authorities produced sufficient money and cooperation to open a postal route through North Carolina to connect Suffolk and Charleston.

Still, by 1774 there was only one post road in the province. It passed through Edenton, Bath, New Bern, and Wilmington. Poor roads and long ferriages across the Albemarle Sound and Pamlico River hindered the post riders who carried the mail each way every two weeks. The postmasters in the towns were unreliable and failed to maintain regular post offices. Letters were carelessly tossed on tables or floors with no regard for the security of the correspondence. Frequently the mail was lost or opened by other parties.

British postal inspector Hugh Finlay in 1774 spent three months in North Carolina attempting to correct the inadequacies of the service. He chastised negligent postmasters and instructed riders in their duties. Finlay arranged for a post office in Brunswick, regular service between Wilmington and Brunswick, and a post between Wilmington and Cross Creek (now Fayetteville), the first east-west route in the province. Nevertheless, on the eve of the Revolution postal service was slow, unreliable, and inefficient. For that matter, so was communication in North Carolina in general.

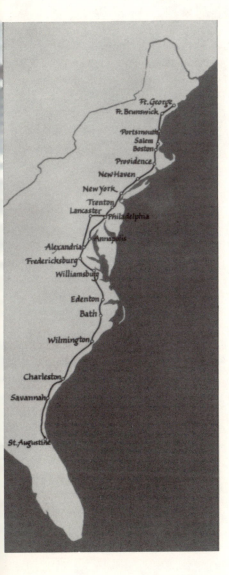

By 1763 there was a post road along the eastern coast of the colonies, and Hugh Finlay's efforts in 1774 to improve postal service in North Carolina, although not entirely successful, resulted in some improvement. Pictured above is a map of Finlay's post road reproduced from the *Iron Worker*, XXXVII, No. 1 (Winter, 1973), 6, and used by permission.

One of the oldest houses in Beaufort is the Hummock House. Other spellings of the name are *Hommack* and *Hammack*; all three are variants derived from the word for hillock. The house stands on ground slightly more elevated than most of Beaufort, and because it was painted white was often called the "White House." The photograph was reproduced by Bob Allen through the courtesy of Roy Eubanks, Beaufort Historical Association.

The Edward Moseley map of 1733 shows the segment of Beaufort Town reproduced here; noted in the legend are "Taylor's House" and "Rich Hummock, NE"; the map appears as Plate 52 of W. P. Cumming, *The Southeast in Early Maps . . .* (Chapel Hill: University of North Carolina Press, c. 1958) and was used in Charles L. Paul, "Colonial Beaufort," *North Carolina Historical Review*, XLII (Spring, 1965), 142.

CHAPTER VI

TOWN LIFE

Today, when almost half of the people in North Carolina reside in towns and cities, it is difficult to realize that there were few more than a dozen towns in the colony. Approximately two percent of the population, or perhaps 5,000 people, lived in urban areas. Compared with other British American colonies North Carolina was slightly less urbanized, but its largest towns did not remotely approximate the populations of Philadelphia, New York, Boston, or Charleston. Indeed, North Carolina was a distinctly rural colony.

The towns of North Carolina developed in response to demands of trade and commerce. In the East they were situated on the best harbor sites in order to take advantage of maritime commerce. In the interior towns appeared on the principal trading routes, especially at the intersection of such thoroughfares, or served as intermediary junctions between western and eastern towns. The importance of these settlements should not be underestimated. They performed an inestimable role in the economic development of the colony.

The oldest town in the province was Bath which was incorporated in 1705. Bath probably contained no more than thirty houses during the colonial period. Although the town was an official port of entry, its commercial importance was limited. Nevertheless, it impressed travelers as a "pretty little place" and contained acceptable lodging facilities.

Beaufort, settled about 1710 and incorporated in 1723, also remained relatively insignificant during the colonial period. It, too, was a port of entry but handled little commerce because of its shallow harbor waters and its remoteness from the ocean. In 1765 a traveler noted that there were no more than twelve houses in Beaufort. The people appeared indolent and subsisted primarily on the abundant fish and oysters found in the area. But during the next ten years Beaufort enjoyed a surge of growth, and in the early 1770s there were at least sixty families living in the town.

Edenton was probably the most pleasant and beautiful town in the province. Located on the northwestern end of the Albemarle Sound and named for Gov. Charles Eden, the town contained some 160 houses and 1,000 inhabitants at the time of the Revolution. Edenton was one of the principal administrative and commercial centers of the province. During the first part of the colonial era the

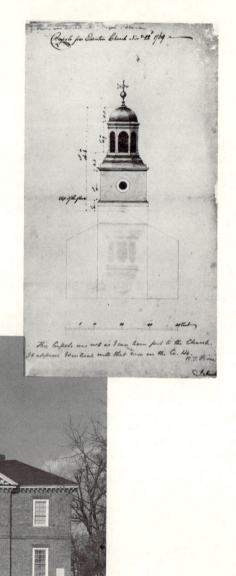

The Chowan County Courthouse, Georgian in style, was built in 1769 and is still in constant use. One of the most impressive in the colonies, the courthouse with its spacious rooms was used for all sorts of occasions in colonial days. In the opinion of R. T. Paine the cupola may have been modeled after a sketch by John Hawks which is preserved in the Hawks Papers. Southern Historical Collection, Chapel Hill, North Carolina. Photograph of courthouse from the files of Division of Archives and History; cupola sketch furnished by Southern Historical Collection.

legislature met regularly in the town and the governors kept residences there. Later Edenton served as the county seat of Chowan County and the location of Lord Granville's land office. It was also a major port. Trade was conducted primarily with the coastal areas and West Indies since the harbor and Pamlico Sound prevented the entrance of large transoceanic vessels. Although Edenton and the Albemarle area were nominally part of North Carolina, the long ferriage over the Albemarle Sound and the poor road facilities tended to isolate the region from the rest of the colony. In fact, before the Revolution the northeastern counties of North Carolina seemed to have maintained closer ties to Virginia in their social and commercial relations.

New Bern, founded by Christopher de Graffenried (Christoph von Graffenried) in 1710 at the junction of the Neuse and Trent rivers, rivaled Wilmington as the largest urban center of the colony by 1775. New Bern developed slowly at first; in 1745 it was no larger than Bath. But by 1765 some 100 buildings and 500 people comprised the town. It continued to increase in population and size, and by the outbreak of the Revolution encompassed a larger geographic area than any other town in the colony.

New Bern's rapid growth resulted from an influx of enterprising merchants in the 1760s who began to tap the interior trade of the colony. Even the Moravians occasionally sent goods to the town for sale. The central coastal location of New Bern eventually led to its selection as the capital of the province, and the permanent placement of government offices and officers in the town further enhanced the commercial possibilities of the area. Although much of New Bern's growth was expansion in the absolute sense, some of it came at the expense of Bath and Beaufort.

Tryon Palace, begun by Governor Tryon in 1767 and completed in 1770, was destroyed by fire after the Revolutionary War. Reconstruction was begun in 1952, and the palace is now recognized as one of the outstanding buildings in the United States. The picture here is after an engraving from Lossing, *The Pictorial Field Book of the Revolution*, II, 364; the engraving was made from drawings by the architect, so this photograph is probably a good representation of the original appearance.

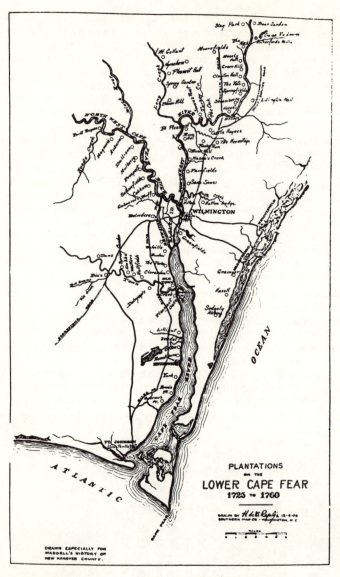

PLANTATIONS
ON THE
LOWER CAPE FEAR
1725 TO 1760

The region along the Cape Fear River and its tributaries, the Northeast and Northwest branches, was settled early by influential men who developed prosperous plantations. Many of these homes are indicated on the map "Plantations on the Lower Cape Fear, 1725 to 1760," drawn by H. de W. Rapely in 1909 especially for use in Alfred Moore Waddell's *History of New Hanover County* (Wilmington: N.P., 1909), facing 39.

In the southeast Brunswick and Wilmington vied for supremacy as commercial centers. Brunswick was founded in 1726 in the process of the settlement of the Cape Fear by the Moore brothers. Beautifully situated high on the west bank of the Cape Fear River and offering the best port facilities in the province, Brunswick should have been in a position to monopolize the trade of the river. However, the Moore family and their allies were opposed in the 1730s by a political faction including Gov. Gabriel Johnston who sponsored the establishment of Wilmington to contest Brunswick's supremacy.

Johnston and his cohorts succeeded in reducing Brunswick to a state of relative unimportance. Wilmington expanded rapidly while Brunswick languished. Nevertheless Brunswick maintained a continuous existence throughout the colonial period. Descendants of the older residents retained their homes in Brunswick. Governors Dobbs and Tryon established their residences at Russellborough just north of the town until 1771 when Tryon moved to his "palace" in New Bern. Finally the "flats," a shallow sandbar across the Cape Fear River above Brunswick and below Wilmington, prevented large, transatlantic vessels from calling at Wilmington without lightering. Some captains preferred to unload their entire cargoes at Brunswick. Thus a corps of merchants and royal customs officials resided in the town to avail themselves of this business. On the eve of the Revolution Brunswick remained a fair-sized town containing some fifty houses. However, during the Revolution the British raided the lower Cape Fear area and the inhabitants of Brunswick abandoned the town.

Wilmington flourished from its inception to become one of the two most populous towns in the province. Originally New Town or New Liverpool, Wilmington thrived under the promotion of the provincial governors. It eventually contained 150 to 200 houses, mostly frame but often two or three stories with double piazzas which were very impressive. Wilmington owed its importance to its port facilities and its successful attempt to divert the back-country trade from Charleston. Numerous Scotch and Scotch-Irish merchants settled in Wilmington and helped to convert the town into the most active center of commerce in North Carolina before the Revolution.

The middle portion of the province contained the towns of Halifax, Tarboro, Cross Creek, and Campbelltown. Halifax was founded in 1757 at the instigation of several merchants who desired to take advantage of the commercial possibilities offered by the Roanoke River traffic. Settlement was delayed slightly by a smallpox epidemic about 1758, but eventually the town contained approximately fifty houses which were mostly of wood or frame construction and painted white. Tarboro was established in 1760 principally to provide Edgecombe County with a satisfactory county seat. Although Tarboro served as a mercantile center, it grew slowly and had only half the population of Halifax.

Fayetteville is the product of two towns which originated in the colonial period. Cross Creek, situated on a tributary of the Northwest Cape Fear by that name, materialized in the 1750s to divert trade from the backcountry. The naturalist William Bartram left a vivid account of the town which was located

> on some heights or swelling hills, from whence the
> creek descends precipitately, then gently meanders
> near a mile . . . to its confluence with the river
> [where men] built mills, which drew people to the
> place who exercised mechanic arts, as smiths, wheel-
> wrights, carpenters, coopers, tanners, etc. And at
> length merchants were encouraged to adventure and
> settle; in short, within eight or ten years from a
> grist-mill, saw-mill, smith-shop and a tavern, arose
> a flourishing commercial town. . . .

The success of Cross Creek spurred a group of men to attempt the establishment of a competing settlement on the river approximately a mile away. In 1762 the assembly incorporated the latter town which was called Campbellton. In 1778 both towns were merged under the name Campbellton which later was changed to Fayetteville.

Western towns included Hillsborough, Salisbury, Salem, and Charlotte. Hillsborough, formerly called Corbin Town and Childs-burgh, was the county seat of Orange County and situated on the Great Wagon Road or Trading Path. In 1764 there were thirty to forty permanent residents in the town including tavern keepers, Scotch merchants, and lawyers.

Salisbury, also on the Trading Path and the county seat of Rowan County, was larger than Hillsborough though smaller than Halifax. After its formal creation in 1755 diverse tradesmen set up their businesses in the town. Within ten years a candlemaker, a doctor, two lawyers, a potter, three hatters, a weaver, a tailor, a butcher, an Indian trader, and a wagon maker, accompanied by numer-ous tavern keepers, had settled in Salisbury. Despite this thriv-ing atmosphere the commerce of Salisbury was distinctly secondary to that of Hillsborough.

The Moravians founded Salem in 1766 to serve as the urban cen-ter of Wachovia. However, it was preceded by two smaller towns, Bethabara and Bethania, which were laid out in 1754 and 1759. For the most part Bethabara contained tradesmen--tailors, shoemakers, carpenters, potters, tanners, millwrights, and gunsmiths--while Bethania was a farming community. By 1766 Bethabara and Bethania contained 88 and 78 inhabitants respectively.

Salem was the product of the usual thoroughness of the Mora-vians who carefully selected a site and planned the settlement of their town. According to H. Roy Merrens the Moravians more than any other settlers meticulously calculated their economic activities and systematically sought the most lucrative commercial markets for their products. The busiest institutions in and around Salem were the pottery, store, tavern, gristmill, and sawmill. The town was an immediate commercial success; it served much of the backcountry of North Carolina, including the Indians who frequently enjoyed the magnanimous hospitality offered by the Moravians.

Charlotte, currently the largest urban community in North Carolina, had an inauspicious beginning. An act of the provincial assembly in 1768 created the town which the legislature hoped would become another center of trade in the backcountry. Although designated the county seat of Mecklenburg County and the site of Queen's College, Charlotte grew slowly. William Moultrie, a South Carolina surveyor, visited the town in 1772 and found a courthouse, jail, tavern, and five or six houses. The importance of the town had yet to materialize.

In addition to these commercial centers of urban development, North Carolina also possessed a complement of smaller, less influential towns. Several were intended as county seats and still exercise that function today--Hertford in Perquimans County, Kinston in Lenoir, Winton in Hertford, Windsor in Bertie, and Elizabethtown in Bladen. Nixonton, in Pasquotank County, was incorporated as a county seat but subsequently lost that distinction. It was, however, a sizable village even at its formal establishment in 1758. Some twenty houses had been built and seventy people resided in the area at that time.

A few towns founded in the colonial period have ceased to function. Johnston, at Mittam's Point on the south side of New River in Onslow County, was incorporated in 1741 but demolished by a hurricane in 1752 and thereafter abandoned. Portsmouth offers an intriguing example of a colonial town which endured for 200 years but has finally succumbed. Established in 1753 near Ocracoke Inlet in Carteret County, Portsmouth was designed as a commercial community to cater to shipping in the Pamlico Sound area. The village of about 500 residents was one of the state's busiest ports before the Civil War, but a threatened Yankee invasion during the conflict caused the populace to evacuate. Only two thirds returned and population thereafter steadily declined. By 1970 only two residents remained amidst a dozen buildings in various states of repair. The village and Portsmouth Island now serve tourists, hunters, and shell collectors.

Urban conditions in colonial North Carolina are best revealed by The Wilmington Town Book, a 1973 published edition of the meetings of the town officials of Wilmington between 1743 and 1778. After the election of the town commissioners by the freeholders, the first order of business in 1743 was to agree to a resurvey of the town lots in order to settle disputes over property boundaries. North Carolinians were a particularly litigious people who happily, it seemed, quarreled over boundary lines and any other matters in rural as well as urban areas. And Wilmington was representative of other towns such as Beaufort which also required periodic assessments of the town boundaries.

Still, Wilmingtonians continued to disregard their property lines. Dr. Moses John DeRosset later complained that James Campbell refused to move his billiard house which was on DeRosset's land. In 1772 the town commissioners issued a list of fifty-eight houses and businesses whose piazzas, balconies, steps, and other structures encroached upon the streets. These included George Moore's stable and poultry house, John Burgwin's tar shed, and John Lyon's tannery. The commissioners imposed an annual rent on all those buildings which interfered with the public right-of-way.

Wilmington residents faced the constant problem of construction and maintenance of streets, alleys, and docks in the city. Twice a year the commissioners demanded that all adult males including slaves meet to effect the necessary construction and repairs. In this respect Wilmington was representative of most North Carolina towns. Yet, the city had a peculiar difficulty in that it was surrounded by sand hills and numerous streams flowed through the town. Drainage proved a constant problem and Wilmingtonians bore the burden of building bridges in their town.

The men of Wilmington seemed habitually to have avoided working on the streets. The town commissioners annually published long lists of defaulters or those who failed to report for street work. Those lists contained thirty to forty names and even included commissioners such as John Rutherfurd, Caleb Mason, and Magnus Cowan, who set a poor example for the townspeople they supposedly served. Defaulters generally received opportunities to remove their obligations. However, if they insisted on remaining delinquent, fines were imposed. Then another difficulty arose. Occasionally the constables who collected the fines found the sums tempting. At least two of those officers of the law absconded with their collections.

Wilmingtonians eventually relieved themselves of the drudgery of building bridges over the streams in the town. After 1772 the commissioners hired workers to construct drainage arches or tunnels, made of brick and timber, over the streams and under the streets. The arches were approximately two feet wide and six and a half feet in height. Portions of the unusual subterranean tunnels still remain visible.

Despite the efforts to promote better drainage, Wilmington streets continued in a state of disrepair. In 1775 Janet Schaw found the streets very muddy. And so it was with all North Carolina towns. Only the very large urban areas of the northern colonies--Boston, Newport, Philadelphia, and New York--had begun paving their streets before the Revolution.

The failure of Wilmington residents to care for the streets was not the only indication of indolence or lack of civic pride. Throughout the colonial era the commissioners passed ordinances to compel the inhabitants of the town to clear the streets, alleys, and docks of dirt, rubbish, and other nuisances. Whites were fined for breaking the law whereas slaves were whipped for their offenses. By 1774 the town was sufficiently populous to justify the appointment of a town scavenger to clean the streets once a week. Apparently the office of trash collector was not wholly desirable. Three men held the position during 1774. Nevertheless, the office of scavenger was not beneath the dignity of Samuel Adams of Boston, Massachusetts, who tactfully fulfilled his duty to the town and enhanced his political prestige among the Bostonians at the same time

When Wilmington citizens failed to fulfill their obligations to help maintain the streets they were listed as defaulters. On this particular list is the name of John Rutherfurd and a notation that "Benjamin Berriman Constable ran away with this money--." Photograph reproduced from Lennon and Kellam, *The Wilmington Town Book*, 61.

The growth of Wilmington from a village to a thriving urban center was reflected not only in the difficulties of street repair and trash removal but also in the problems of traffic control. Eventually ordinances were passed to prevent persons from riding "immoderately or uncommonly fast" through the streets, conducting races in the streets, and keeping "unruly horses" in the town. In the larger cities of the northern colonies traffic accidents occasionally took the lives of innocent bystanders. Wilmington intended to protect its residents, and the commissioners often levied fines against the lawbreakers. Traffic problems were not unique to Wilmington. Salisbury also had difficulty with persons driving wildly through its streets with unloaded carts and wagons, while Carteret County court levied a fine against persons for racing in the streets of Beaufort.

Large urban communities also faced the constant threat of fire. Houses which were clustered together contributed to a rapid spread of flames, particularly when many were frame with daub and wooden chimneys and wooden shingles. Such structures caught fire easily and blazed fiercely. Wilmington experienced at least three major fires during the eighteenth century--in 1756, 1775, and 1785 or 1786.

The danger of fire arose from many sources in Wilmington. Fires on the wharves for boiling pitch and tar and on the streets for burning rubbish caused great concern. Eventually the commissioners banned such fires after sunset. They also ordered that all hay, straw, fodder, and oakum stored in residences be removed in hopes that the elimination of the flammable material would reduce the risk of fire.

83

In the Tryon Palace is this eighteenth century English brown leather
fire bucket embellished with an
elaborate coat of arms. Most home-
owners had buckets just as functional
but simpler. Photograph from the
files of the Division of Archives and
History.

Sooty chimneys probably caused most of the fires in the town
and fire prevention centered on the chimneys of the houses and kitchens of the residents. The commissioners required that all chimneys be at least three feet above the highest part of the roof in
order that sparks be extinguished before settling on the roofs.
Fines were imposed on those persons whose chimneys caught fire.
However, the fines did not spur the townspeople to clean their chimneys and the commissioners finally ordered every resident to sweep
his chimneys from top to bottom every two weeks. Later the time
period for cleaning chimneys was extended to twenty days for kitchen
fireplaces throughout the year and for all fireplaces between Octobe
and April. An attempt to hire a town chimneysweep failed. Furthermore, the regulations were ineffective; fines continued to be impose
for chimney fires.

Wilmington also developed a program for fighting fires. Taxes
were levied to purchase leather fire buckets and ladders for public
use. The commissioners loaned these items to citizens for private
use, and to their dismay the townspeople often failed to return the
borrowed items. Such negligence eventually evoked ordinances re-
stricting the use of public property for private benefit. Additional laws required each Wilmingtonian housekeeper to purchase one
or more water buckets. Again, Wilmingtonians ignored the law. The
commissioners continually reminded the people to obtain the necessary fire buckets.

The preeminent piece of firefighting equipment in the town as the fire engine. A special property tax--as opposed to the usual poll tax--was placed on the houses in Wilmington for the purchase of the engine. The commissioners in 1755 engaged Benjamin Heron to procure the machine in London. Fortunately, Wilmingtonians had little need for their engine because the equipment failed to receive the constant supervision and repair which it needed. By 1772 the fire engine had so greatly deteriorated that the town decided to buy a newer, larger model. The commissioners intended to sell the older engine but later determined to have it repaired so that it would "throw water an equal distance of a New Engine." Within eighteen months the new engine had arrived from Philadelphia. Apparently neither of the fire engines was utilized to combat the 1775 fire.

Statutes relating to other towns in the province indicated a similar concern about fire hazards. For example, wooden chimneys were forbidden in Halifax and New Bern, while the commissioners of Edenton in 1756 received legislative approval to levy a tax on the residents of the town for the purchase of a fire engine. The Moravian records show that several small fires prompted the appointment of fire inspectors in Bethabara in 1759 and in Salem in 1773. The inhabitants of Bethabara regularly cleaned their chimneys during the years before the Revolution; Salem obtained the services of a chimney sweep.

The large slave population in Wilmington constituted another overriding concern to the white citizenry. By the end of the colonial era as many as fifty percent of the town residents were slaves and the town commissioners passed numerous ordinances to restrict the activities of the blacks. The first such town law forbade white inhabitants of Wilmington to rent any house in the town to slaves. Later, ordinances prohibited slaves from engaging in any commercial enterprise in the town unless they possessed written permission from their masters. Additional ordinances placed curfews on slaves of nine and ten o'clock in the evenings depending upon the season of the year. Penalties were also prescribed for slaves who created disturbances within the town limits. Finally, whites were not permitted to sell rum to slaves, hire slaves, or purchase merchandise from slaves without the consent of their owners.

These town ordinances and their subsequent enforcement reflected the urban circumstances of slaves. Apparently some slaves led a partially liberated existence. They earned money by selling and trading merchandise as well as by hiring themselves as part-time or full-time workers on a daily, weekly, or monthly basis. For a fee they could obtain a house, tenement, or outbuilding for their private lodging. Thus, the slaves enjoyed a degree of freedom, a situation which caused anxiety among the whites, who lived in constant fear of slave uprisings.

Another major concern in Wilmington was the sale of meat and produce. Originally the area below the courthouse served as the marketplace for the town, but during the 1740s a separate market house was constructed. In order to give all town residents an equal opportunity to purchase produce the commissioners ordered that all goods be sold at the market house until ten o'clock in the morning at which time they could be vended about the streets. The public received further protection by laws which prohibited the sale of unwholesome meat and diluted milk. Tables establishing the size, weight, and price of bread prevented bakers from taking unfair advantage of their customers, while maximum prices for beef provided consumer protection in the purchase of that commodity. Similar ordinances passed by the commissioners of New Bern showed equal concern for the public welfare. In that town retailers of grain, dairy, and poultry products were prohibited from buying in the market until nine o'clock so that housekeepers might have the first opportunity to purchase the produce which they desired. Moreover, evasion of the market laws by purchase of produce before it reached the town on market days was forbidden.

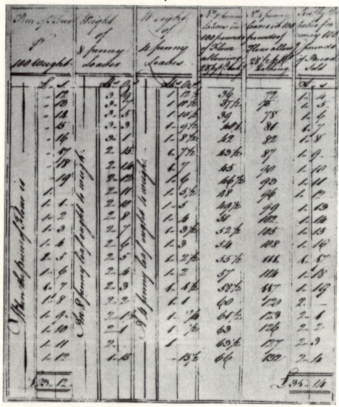

In 1768 the Wilmington town commissioners approved this "Table of the Assize of Loaf Bread" in an effort to regulate marketing practices. Photograph reproduced from Lennon and Kellam, *The Wilmington Town Book*, 179.

The variety of other business which occupied the attention of
e Wilmington town commissioners is intriguing. In 1752 several
pposedly rabid dogs terrorized the inhabitants of the town; in
63 materials were purchased to make a cushion and slipcover for
e pulpit of St. James Church; in 1768 workmen were hired to sink
o wells near the courthouse for the use of the public; in 1773
e commissioners rebuked the owners of open necessary houses which
fronted the public; and in 1774 the town purchased a ducking stool
 device which Edenton had deemed necessary in 1767) for the punish-
nt of prostitutes, gossips, scolds, and brawlers. Yet, despite
ese evidences of urban living, the town retained a distinctly
ral flavor as did all colonial towns in America. Poultry flitted
out, hogs and goats ran loose, and horses and cattle wandered
mlessly about the streets. The distinction between town and
untry life in many ways was insignificant.

On this page are pictured two rooms in Tryon Palace. The furnishings
in the dining room are appropriate English eighteenth century antiques;
the dining room was designed and painted to match the doorway, which is
from an eighteenth century English home. (Photograph by Louis H. Frohman.)
The governor's bedroom is also handsomely furnished with authentic furniture
suitable for a colonial "palace." Photograph from files of the Division of
Archives and History.

CHAPTER VII

CONCLUSION

Colonial North Carolina society constituted a kaleidoscopic arrangement of languages, religions, and life-styles. It was a product of European culture developed in a New World environment. The American wilderness modified elements of the Old World and often evoked new societal forms. Still, the colonials clung tenaciously to their European past and imitated their European contemporaries whenever possible.

A noteworthy facet of Carolina society was the varied backgrounds of the settlers. Indians were supplanted by Europeans and Africans. The whites originated primarily in England but large contingents represented such continental countries as France, Germany, Switzerland, Ireland, and Scotland. The blacks came from various west African states, especially the Guinea Coast, and from the West Indies.

One aspect of European society which was imported by the dominant white colonials was a hierarchal class structure. The utilization of slavery and indentured servitude reinforced the class system. The greatest extremes of wealth appeared in the Albemarle and particularly the lower Cape Fear area. Nevertheless, North Carolinians seemed much less differentiated than the people of most other English colonies along the seaboard.

The manner of living in North Carolina reflected Old World habits tempered by the New World frontier. Primitive conditions characterized frontier life; and a near subsistence economy prevailed throughout much of the province. Many, however, accumulated capital which permitted a life of relative ease, even luxury, for some of the colonials. Wealth was a major factor in the determination of modes of housing, standards of dress, opportunities for education, and attitudes toward cultural enrichment.

The religious experience of North Carolinians similarly reflected varying attitudes. The Anglican church or Church of England was the established church, but it competed less than successfully with numerous other Protestant groups. The diversity of denominational sentiment contributed to a spirit of toleration on the part of the sectaries. Obviously no one denomination could predominate, and all were forced to adopt a policy of tolerance.

89

Transportation and communication were largely dictated by geo graphical considerations. Numerous watercourses and the marshy, sandy soil of the eastern portion of the province hindered the progress of transportation. A sparse population compounded such difficulties. However, continuous westward settlement and an increased populace promoted a serviceable transportation network by the outbreak of the Revolution. Communication was similarly delayed. Postal facilities arrived late in the colonial period, while the printing press and newspaper also made tardy appearances Before the Revolution transportation and communication were generally slow, inefficient, and expensive.

Although North Carolina was predominantly rural, towns--more accurately, villages, in many cases--developed in response to commercial demands. Such towns were often the result of private promotional endeavors, but some were instigated by the colonial government which assumed responsibility for encouraging commerce within the province. Town life presented problems of a modern nature including rubbish removal, sewage disposal, traffic control, fire prevention, and law enforcement. Towns promoted cultural advancement by clustering individuals in a small geographical area which facilitated social interaction and fostered an interchange of ideas. Nevertheless, like most English colonials, North Carolinians remained basically a rural people.

REFERENCES FOR ADDITIONAL READING

Allcott, John V. *Colonial Homes in North Carolina.*
Raleigh: Carolina Charter Tercentenary Commission,
1963.

Anscombe, Francis C. *I Have Called You Friends. The
Story of Quakerism in North Carolina.* Boston:
Christopher Publishing House, 1959.

Bassett, John Spencer. *Slavery and Servitude in the
Colony of North Carolina.* Baltimore: Johns Hopkins
Press, 1896.

Boyd, William K., ed. *William Byrd's Histories of the
Dividing Line betwixt Virginia and North Carolina.*
Raleigh: North Carolina Historical Commission, 1929.

Brickell, John. *The Natural History of North Carolina.*
Murfreesboro, N.C.: Johnson Publishing Company, 1968.
First published, Dublin, 1737.

Brooks, Jerome. *Green Leaf and Gold: Tobacco in North
Carolina.* Raleigh: State Department of Archives and
History, 1962.

Cathey, Cornelius C. *Agriculture in North Carolina Before
the Civil War.* Raleigh: State Department of Archives
and History, 1966.

Clark, Walter, ed. *The State Records of North Carolina.*
16 vols. (XI-XXVI). Winston, Goldsboro: State of
North Carolina, 1895-1914.

Connor, R. D. W. *History of North Carolina: The Colonial
and Revolutionary Periods.* Chicago: Lewis Publishing
Company, 1919.

Craig, James H. *The Arts and Crafts in North Carolina,
1689-1840.* Winston-Salem: Museum of Early Southern
Decorative Arts, Old Salem, Inc., 1965.

Crittenden, Charles Christopher. *The Commerce of North
Carolina, 1763-1789.* New Haven: Yale University
Press, 1936.

Fries, Adelaide L., ed. *Records of the Moravians in North
Carolina.* Vols. I, II. Raleigh: North Carolina
Historical Commission, 1922; reprinted 1968.

Hall, Clement. *A Collection of Many Christian Experiences,
Sentences, and Several Places of Scripture Improved.*
Introduction by William S. Powell. Raleigh: State
Department of Archives and History, 1961. First
published, New Bern, 1753.

Hooker, Richard, ed. *The Carolina Backcountry on the Eve
of the Revolution: The Journal and Other Writings
of Charles Woodmason, Anglican Itinerant.* Chapel
Hill: University of North Carolina Press, 1953.

Johnson, Guion G. *Ante-Bellum North Carolina: A Social History*. Chapel Hill: University of North Carolina Press, 1937.

Johnston, Frances Benjamin, and Thomas T. Waterman. *The Early Architecture of North Carolina*. Chapel Hill: University of North Carolina Press, 1941.

Knight, Edgar W. *Public School Education in North Carolina*. Boston: Houghton Mifflin Co., 1916.

Lee, E. Lawrence. *The Lower Cape Fear in Colonial Days*. Chapel Hill: University of North Carolina Press, 1965.

Lefler, Hugh T., and Albert R. Newsome. *North Carolina. The History of a Southern State*. Third edition. Chapel Hill: University of North Carolina Press, 1973.

Lefler, Hugh T., and William S. Powell. *Colonial North Carolina. A History*. New York: Charles Scribner's Sons, 1973.

Lennon, Donald R., and Ida Brooks Kellam, eds. *The Wilmington Town Book, 1743-1778*. Raleigh: Division of Archives and History, 1973.

Leyburn, James G. *The Scotch-Irish. A Social History*. Chapel Hill: University of North Carolina Press, 1962.

McRee, Griffith J., ed. *Life and Correspondence of James Iredell, One of the Associate Justices of the Supreme Court of the United States*. 2 vols. New York: D. Appleton and Co., 1857-1858.

Merrens, H. Roy. *Colonial North Carolina in the Eighteenth Century*. Chapel Hill: University of North Carolina Press, 1964.

Meyer, Duane. *The Highland Scots of North Carolina, 1732-1776*. Chapel Hill: University of North Carolina Press, 1961.

Morgan, Jacob L., *et. al. History of the Luthern Church in North Carolina*. Salisbury: United Evangelical Lutheran Synod of North Carolina, 1953.

Paschal, George W. *History of North Carolina Baptists*. 2 vols. Raleigh: General Board, North Carolina Baptist State Convention, 1930-1955.

Paschal, Herbert R., Jr. *History of Colonial Bath*. Raleigh: Edwards and Broughton, 1955.

Ramsey, Robert W. *Carolina Cradle, Settlement of the Northwest Carolina Frontier, 1747-1762*. Chapel Hill: University of North Carolina Press, 1964.

Rights, Douglas. *The American Indian in North Carolina*. Durham: Duke University Press, 1947. Reprinted, Winston-Salem: J. F. Blair, 1957.

Saunders, William L., ed. *The Colonial Records of North Carolina*. 10 vols. Raleigh: State of North Carolina, 1886-1890.

Schaw, Janet. *Journal of a Lady of Quality*. Edited by Evangeline W. Andrews with the collaboration of Charles M. Andrews. New Haven: Yale University Press, 1921.

Schoepf, Johann David. *Travels in the Confederation, 1783-1784*. 2 vols. Translated and edited by Alfred J. Morrison. Philadelphia: W. J. Campbell, 1911.

Smyth, John Ferdinand Dalziel. *A Tour in the United States of America*. 2 vols. Dublin: Price, Moncrieffe, 1784.

South, Stanley A. *Indians in North Carolina*. Raleigh: State Department of Archives and History, 1959.

Sweet, William Warren. *Men of Zeal. The Romance of American Methodist Beginnings*. New York: Abingdon Press, 1935.